The
WOMAN'S DAY
CRÊPE COOKBOOK

The WOMAN'S DAY CRÊPE COOKBOOK

by

Sylvia Schur
Creative Food Service, Inc.

A FAWCETT BOOK

Fawcett Publications, Inc., Greenwich, Connecticut

Contents

Introduction

You are always able to serve a meal or a snack in style, when you know how to make crêpes . . . the sublime pancakes. Lighter and more delicate than sturdy flapjacks, crêpes hold fillings from savory to sweet, for appetizer, main dish, or dessert.

Pancakes were our first bread, baked on the girdle of hot stones which surrounded the fire, and then called griddlecakes. Earliest cookbooks refer to pancakes, and Shrove Tuesday came to be known as Pancake Day in England many centuries ago. All the eggs and fats in the home were used up in pancakes, eaten during the merriment preceding Lent. The bell which summoned people to church became known as the Pancake Bell.

To this day, in the town of Olney, an annual ladies' Pancake Day race starts at 11:55 A.M. Each contestant wears an apron and a hat, and carries a pan with a pancake in it. At the starting bell, she tosses her pancake in the air, catches it in the pan, and is off on a 415-yard dash to the village churchyard, where the first arrival is kissed by the ringer of the Pancake Bell. Legend has it that this race was first run more than 500 years ago, when a housewife heard the Shriving Bell summoning her to church, and dashed off to the services with her pancake pan still in her hand . . .

a tale which tells a lot about the speed and versatility of pancake or crêpe making.

French and Belgian cooks called the pancake a crêpe, and made many regional versions, increasing the eggs for lighter cakes. In the nineteenth century, chefs experimented with flavoring nuances, and the most famous crêpe dessert of all, Crêpes Suzette, was an accidental result. One story has it that Henri Charpentier, chef at the Monte Carlo, planned a crêpe dessert for a dinner ordered by the Prince of Wales, whose guests included a young girl named Suzette. The chef had prepared a special orange-and-liqueur-flavored sauce in advance. When he heated the sauce, it accidentally flamed, to Charpentier's chagrin. As the flames died down, he tasted the sauce and found it needed no salvaging, but in fact was improved, and so he served it forthwith. Asked for the name, he dubbed his triumph Crêpes Princess, but the Prince renamed the dish in honor of Suzette, and so it has been called ever since. Unless, of course, you believe a different story, placed a few years later, in 1897, when a star of the Comédie Française played the part of a maid named Suzette, who served crêpes in the course of her role. The pancakes for the part were supplied by Chef Joseph of the Restaurant Marivaux, and he is said to have prepared the orange-sugar sauce named Suzette in her honor. Or his may have been another version of the Charpentier recipe, which is still being changed by inventive chefs today!

Crêpes in Many Languages

Crêpes appear in the cuisines of many lands, made with the flour most typical of the area, filled with favorite combinations of local foods. You can enjoy crêpes from wafer-thin to thick and puffy in different parts of France, made with butter in the North, and with oil in the South. Or sample Russian Blini made with buckwheat flour and filled with caviar or a salty herring mixture. Or prepare ethereal Hungarian Palascinta filled with cinnamon-raisin sweetened cheese, then baked under a blanket of sour cream or melted butter, or filled with apricot or strawberry preserves and topped with whipped cream before serving. Enjoy light white Chinese pancakes filled with savory duck in plum sauce, or hearty tortilla crêpes sweet with masa, filled with chili or taco-sauced meat. CRÊPES ARE COMPATIBLE. They fit in with your menu needs. Welcome guests with appetizer crêpes, or serve crêpes as a main course, as a dessert to round out a light meal, or as a snack any time. Fillings can be as simple as banana and whipped cream, or preserves and a sprinkling of confectioners' sugar, or ice cream and chocolate sauce—as elegant as Sole Mousse Crêpes or Crêpes Cordon Bleu or Gâteau aux Crêpes Meringuées. Take your pick of hundreds of crêpe variations given here, to match your mood, your budget, your time, or your taste. Or use any pie filling for a crêpe—it's easier than pie!

Crêpes Are Convenient

Prepare crêpes at the last minute; or make them a few hours ahead and let them stand until serving time; or make them well in advance, wrap and freeze them for future use. Serve crêpes individually or heated in a casserole, serve them simply or dramatically flamed at the table. You can re-heat crêpes in a pan, or in the oven, or under the grill, or in a microwave oven.

Most crêpes are at their best piping hot, even with cool filling—for example, hot blini with chilled caviar and sour cream. But some crêpes, filled with cheese or salad or with sweet creamy mixtures for dessert, are also good cold. Roll cold crêpes into cylinders, for easy eat-out-of-hand party fare.

CRÊPES ARE ECONOMICAL. They help stretch small amounts of fillings to make hearty servings, and the batter itself is inexpensive to make.

Given a few eggs, a cup of flour, and a cup of milk or water—ingredients generally at hand—crêpes can feed a crowd, wrapping up whatever you have available or left over, or extending expensive ingredients, for elegant results with more style than money. It takes little to fill a crêpe—about 2 tablespoons of most fillings, or up to ¼ cup for a plump rolled crêpe. Yet when these fillings are wrapped in a satisfying crêpe, they give one a real sense of well-being.

Crêpes Are Accommodating

Crêpes can be made with one egg or three, for a batter with more or less lightness. If you add extra egg yolk to the batter, it will be creamier and smoother of texture. If you make yours with egg whites only, the crêpes will be a little tougher, and lighter in color. Offset this with a tablespoon of oil per egg white.

The liquid used for crêpes can be water or milk, or half of each; or cream or buttermilk or beer. Or add a spoonful of club soda for extra lightness. You will even find a rich batter made with eggnog here. Water makes tender crêpes; milk and part cream make a rich and satisfying batter; cream makes still richer crêpes; buttermilk or beer or club soda makes very light crêpes.

Use the flour you have on hand, or even a pancake mix, as indicated in the recipes which follow. Cornstarch, whole wheat flour, rice flour, and buckwheat are more hygroscopic, absorb more water, than all-purpose flour. Batter made with these flours may need a little more liquid or an extra egg to make a delicately thin crêpe. Butter adds flavor as well as "shortness" to the batter; oil can be used as well. If you clarify the butter,* thus eliminating the milk solids, your crêpes will be more even in color, with fewer brown spots. Sugar increases browning while it sweetens the crêpes, as does liqueur. If the batter for crêpes rests at room temperature for a half hour or more—or better yet, if it is stored 24 hours or up to a week or more in the refrigerator, the starch in the flour is more completely hydrolyzed, the gluten strands form more elastic links, and your crêpes, although tender, light-textured, and thin, will be easy to handle. This is why recipes read: "Let stand 30 minutes or longer." If you do not have time to wait, you can make crêpes immediately; they just won't be quite as light in texture. A batch of crêpe batter premixed in a pitcher or a pour-measure is an asset in the refrigerator. This keeps well for a week or more, ready to fill in for meals, and to add a special touch to quick meals, from breakfast to midnight snacks. Refrigerated batter may thicken slightly or become thinner on standing. To restore consistency, add a little more liquid, or a little more flour. Or add a different flour and an extra egg, or seasoning, to make crêpe surprises for many meals, with new interest and no repetitions.

Crêpes Are Chic and Versatile

—in whatever style you choose to make them. You can play the crêpes game with any of 24 different batters from classic light French through tasty fines herbes, or sweet chocolate, or sourdough or new low cholesterol crêpes. Choose from more than 200 different fillings, from appetizer seafood mixtures to souffléed dessert crêpes or cool crêpes with mousse fillings.

---

*To clarify butter: Place butter in a small, deep pan and bring quickly to a boil. Let stand a minute for foam to settle. Skim foam from surface, pour off clear golden clarified butter oil, leaving the milk solids which settle at the bottom of the pan.

Any filling could go in any crêpe wrapper, and you could serve crêpes made from one batter with a different filling every day of the year. But why wrap guacamole in a French crêpe when we give you a tortilla crêpe recipe?
Tip: For a delectable omelet, add a little of any crêpe batter to eggs, beat, then cook as usual.

Choosing a Crêpe Pan

You can make a crêpe in any frying pan, or on a flat griddle, but a flat-bottomed crêpe pan, or an inverted domed pan especially designed for the purpose, will help you do a better job. The following list is a guide to the pros and cons of crêpe pans from least expensive to truly luxurious. You can make a good crêpe on any of them; some make it easier for you, and each type has its ardent adherents!

Choosing and Seasoning a Crêpe Pan

A pan with a bottom about 6 inches in diameter makes a practical crêpe; two identical pans, used side by side, cut the cooking time required in half. Whatever crêpe pan you choose, careful seasoning or breaking-in is a major factor in achieving good results. Reserve your crêpe pan only for crêpes or omelets. Season or break in a new or washed or long-unused pan by heating oil in the pan. Let it stand 1 hour or longer, then pour off oil, wipe the pan with a paper towel, and heat butter in the pan. Pour off excess, reserving it for later crêpes, and proceed with making crêpes. Wipe pan with paper towel between uses, and rub with a little coarse salt, if necessary, to remove any fragments which cling to the pan. Scour with soap and water as rarely as practical, and reseason the pan after each washing. Preheat before each use. Some pans will darken with use, and will then conduct heat and brown crêpes better than ever.

Pan Types, Multipurpose and Special

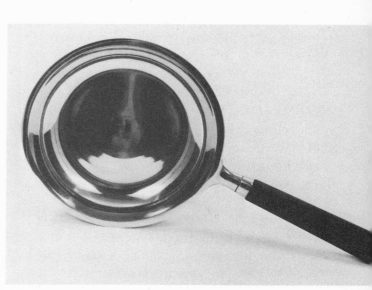

CAST-IRON SKILLET
Wagner or other brand
About $6

Browns well, holds heat evenly, but is somewhat heavy to handle for spreading the batter and for flipping crêpes. May tend to darken crêpes excessively if heat is not carefully controlled. Avoid scouring, reseason often. Prepare crêpes as in Basic Directions (page 17).

LOW-SIDED FRENCH CRÊPE PAN
Varied import names
About $6 to $20

These are made of sheet iron or polished heavy aluminum; some have wooden handles which remain cool during cooking. Flat base and low sides simplify shaping thin crêpes as pan is tilted; shape is designed for ease in flipping crêpes. Use same break-in procedure as suggested for iron pans; the polished heavy aluminum maintains finish and requires little breaking in. It is expensive, but gives long wear. Prepare crêpes as in Basic Directions (page 17).

HEAVY-DUTY ALUMINUM OMELET PAN
$6.59 to $12.95

This is a convenient and practical pan, although the curved sides may not produce symmetrical crêpes. Season according to directions (page 9); easy to use and care for. Prepare crêpes as in Basic Directions (page 17).

TEFLON-COATED ALUMINUM PAN, WOODEN HANDLE
$5.50 to $6.50

This too is a practical pan, and the wooden handle is easy to hold. Reduce the amount of butter used in this pan or the crêpes may slide from the pan too rapidly when you lift them. Prepare crêpes as in Basic Directions (page 17).

COPPER CRÊPE PAN
About $25

Season briefly. Copper conducts heat rapidly, so reduce the heat as soon as the pan is hot. Makes delicate, well-browned crêpes. Requires polishing outside after use. Inside tin finish is delicate. Avoid cleaning with harsh abrasives. Prepare crêpes as in Basic Directions (page 17).

POPEIL'S CRÊPE MAGICIAN
Popeil Brothers, Inc.
2323 West Pershing Road
Chicago, Illinois 60609
$9.95 includes pan,
recipe book, freezer
container

Heavy-duty die-cast aluminum, 7½-inch diameter, curved surface pan has Teflon non-stick coating, is grooved on bottom for even heating. Pouring lip on each side carries off any excess batter. Plastic handle with hang-up knob simplifies holding and storage.

Preparation for pan: Wipe with damp cloth, place on range, and add cooking oil just to cover bottom of pan. Heat oil over medium heat until it begins to smoke. Turn off heat, let stand 1 hour or longer. Pour off oil, wipe pan with paper towel.

Directions for use: Pour batter into preheated pan; pour off excess. Return pan to heat for 15 to 30 seconds or until surface of crêpe is dry and edge slightly browned. Turn pan over and tap crêpe out. No butter is used for the pan itself. One tablespoon additional butter is suggested in some crêpe recipes for this pan.

THE CRÊPE MAKER   Taylor & Ng of San Francisco,
San Francisco, California
$12.50 with booklet

Steel pan, 8-inch diameter, designed for dipping into the batter; holes around outer rim for heat dispersion. Pan comes covered with machine oil; requires seasoning before use. Handle is a raw wood; assembled after purchase; and remains cool during cooking.

Preparation of pan: Scrub with cleanser, steel wool, and hot water. Rinse well and dry. Rub oil on inside and out, heat pan over low heat. Increase heat to medium for 5 to 10 minutes, repeating rubbing with oil. Clean with paper towels after use; pan darkens with use.

Directions for use: Grease the pan and heat it thoroughly, but not too hot. Invert it and dip in batter placed in shallow dinner plate. Practice is needed here: if pan is too hot, the batter falls back in the plate partially cooked; if pan is too cool or too oily, batter does not adhere. Place batter-coated pan over heat, upside down, to cook crêpes in 1 to 2 minutes. Peel crêpe off pan, grease again, and repeat. Crêpe makers who begin with this pan and learn to handle it find results effective and practical.

Disadvantages: Heat of pan must be judged accurately, or crêpes won't form. There is some unevenness in browning, particularly over gas flame. Only one side browns, although crêpes cook through without turning.

CRÊPES 'N THINGS NORDIC CRÊPE PAN   Northland Aluminum
Products, Inc.
Minneapolis, Minnesota
55416
$15 includes recipe book

Cast-aluminum pan, 8-inch diameter, with nonstick coating. Wooden handle is designed so pan can fit over 9-inch pie pan for dipping. Lightweight, partitioned inside for even heating.

Preparation of pan: Wash with mild detergent, rinse, and dry. Coat domed bottom surface with vegetable shortening. Place on low heat until fat melts. Remove excess fat with paper toweling. Allow pan to remain on low heat approximately 5 minutes.

Directions for use: Dip oiled and heated pan into batter, invert it, and place over heat. Cook until underside of crêpe is browned and upper surface dry. Remove the crêpe with fork or spatula. Dip pan in batter again and repeat process. Crêpes cook uniformly, but brown on one side only.

THE CRÊPE MAKER

Made in Japan, importer, Alfred E. Knobler & Co. Inc. Moonachie, New Jersey 07074 $13.50 includes recipe book

Heavy-gauge aluminum 8-inch diameter pan with 9-inch wooden handle, eye to attach string for hanging.

Preparation of pan: Wash with mild detergent. Wipe with vegetable oil. Place over low heat for 30 minutes. Wipe with paper towel.

Directions for use: Dip preheated crêpe maker, curved side down, into batter; lift immediately. Turn curved side up, cook 20 to 30 seconds. Loosen the crêpe with a fork, then turn the pan over to release the crêpe. This crêpe will be cooked through, but browned on only one side.

PORTABLE CRÊPE GRIDDLE— BUTANE-HEATED $100

This French import has a flat butane-heated disk, about 10 inches in diameter. It requires seasoning and preheating, then turns out large, thin crêpes so speedily that they can be prepared to order on the spot for a party.

CRÊPES MACHINE

Hammacher Schlemmer Catalogue 147 East 57th Street New York, New York $595

This French import rolls out crêpes enough to keep up with demand in a specialty crêpe restaurant, each crêpe lacy-thin and uniform in size and color. Not worth the investment, unless you have an enormous family who love crêpes, entertain on a big scale and often, or run a restaurant, camp, school, or resort.

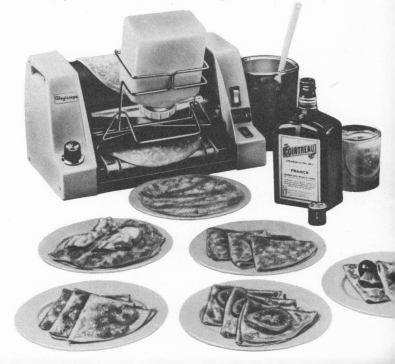

CRÊPES-PLUS   Ekco Housewares Co.
                      Franklin Park, Illinois
                      $9.95 to $12.95

Stainless-steel upside-down type, available in 7- or 8-inch diameter with plastic handle. Pan can double, right side up, as a skillet.

Preparation for pan: Slow seasoning not necessary.

Directions for use: Preheat pan with fat for 5 minutes, invert and dip in batter for a second, turn and cook directly over burner until edges turn light brown: flip onto plate. Care must be taken with pan; crêpes can burn in spots.

CONTEMPRA   Contempra Industries, Inc.
AUTOMATIC   371 Essex Road
ELECTRIC   New Shrewsbury, N.J. 07753
CREPE MAKER   Price: $24.95 includes
(Model C-100)   recipe booklet

Heat resistant plastic body, 7½-inch diameter with Teflon* II domed cooking surface. Plastic handle encases timed thermostatic temperature control. Plugs into regular household current, free standing. Heating unit is completely encased, weighs under 2 pounds.

Preparation of pan: Before first use, wipe cooking surface with oil-soaked paper towel. Pan is at cooking temperature when red signal lights.

Directions for use: Pour batter into a large pie or dinner plate. Plug in pan. Wait for red light. Dip inverted pan into batter, tilt slightly to remove excess batter, then turn pan over and let stand. Red light will be off. In less than one minute, light will return. Remove crepe by inverting over a warmed plate.

LA CRÊPE-ETTE   General Housewares Corp.
AUTHENTIQUE   Cookware Group
                      P.O. Box 4066
                      Terre Haute, Indiana 47804
                      $12.99 includes
                              recipes on hang tag

Cast-iron skillet with 9-inch diameter. Shape of pan is like a top hat that has been collapsed to create a circular plateau in the center surrounded by a well. This shaping aids in maintaining uniform shape of crêpe. No need to tilt pan to spread batter. Crêpes brown lightly and evenly.

Preparation for pan: Although preseasoned, slow seasoning is recommended.

Directions for use: Preheat seasoned pan with grease. Pour batter onto plateau area. Cook until edges are lightly browned.

Advantage: Lifting of pan is minimized by the unique feature of the pan.

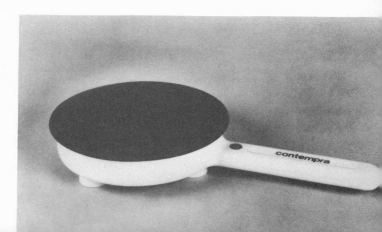

CRÊPE MASTER Atlas Metal Spinning Co.
South San Francisco, California
$15 includes recipe book

Upside-down-type steel crêpe pan, with an 8-inch diameter and finished wood handle. A wheel-like cast-iron ring serves as a base for the pan, allows for equal heat distribution. The inside of the crêpe pan is hollow.

Preparation for pan: Wash off machine oil that acts as a preservative, season according to directions in Seasoning a Crêpe Pan (page 9).

Directions for use: Place ring on heating element, pan directly on top. Grease pan, preheat. Invert and dip pan into plate filled with batter. Prepare crêpes as in Basic Directions (page 17).

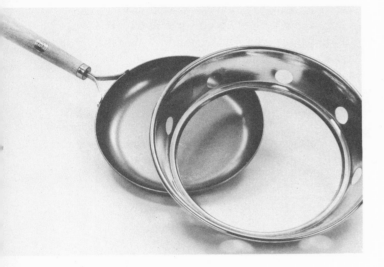

CRÊPE PAN Copco, Inc.
11 East 26th Street
New York, New York 10010
$18

Porcelain enamel-covered cast-iron skillet with sloped edge and 7½-inch diameter allows for even heating of iron and easy cleaning surface. Handle is cast iron. A very flat base and sides make this pan similar to classic French crêpe pans.

Preparation for pan: Slow seasoning not recommended. Preheat gently.

Directions for use: Prepare crêpes according to Basic Directions (page 17).

ELECTRIC CRÊPE PAN Grandinetti
P.O. Box 160
2815 Los Flores Boulevard
Lynwood, California 90262
Under $30 includes
recipe booklet

Cast aluminum, 8-inch diameter; domed surface is nonstick-coated. Plastic wood-grained handle encases thermostatically controlled electric wiring. Plugs into regular household current. Pan is free-standing, for ease in preheating. Heating element molded into aluminum pan allows for even browning of crêpes.

Preparation for pan: Heat until water drops dance on pan. This pan requires no preseasoning. Wipe with butter, using a paper towel.

Directions for use: Pour batter into a large dinner plate. Dip inverted pan into batter, tilt slightly to remove excess batter, then turn pan over and let stand. Allow crêpe to cook until lightly browned around edges. Invert pan over warmed plate and loosen crêpe with fork.

Advantage: Uniform temperature; no variation due to removal from heat source or build-up of heat. Cooks uniform crêpes.

ROUND GRIDDLE PAN Leyse Aluminum Company Kewaunee, Wisconsin 54216 $7.95 or $8.95

Heavy-gauge aluminum flat round disk, 12-inch diameter with aluminum handle. Even heat distribution. Available at a higher cost with Teflon II® coating.

Preparation for pan: Requires seasoning according to directions in Seasoning a Crêpe Pan (page 9).

Directions for use: Preheat seasoned pan. Pour batter slowly into center. Tilt griddle to ease spreading. Cook until lightly brown, remove with a fork or flip pan over, releasing crêpe onto dish.

Advantage: Allows you to make any size crêpe, depending on the amount of batter poured.

LA CRÊPE COMPLETE HOOVER ELECTRIC CRÊPE MAKER/ MODEL B3087 The Hoover Company North Canton, Ohio 44760 Price: $24.99 includes instruction book and ¼ cup measure

Die cast aluminum 8-inch pan with Rockbottom™ non-stick cooking surface. Temperature control dial plugs into side of footed pan to give pan complete electric control from warm to 425°F. A red light signals end of preheating time. A cord clip prevents accidental tipping of the crêpe pan.

Preparation of pan: Wash pan (without control), rinse and dry. Season by brushing 2 tablespoons oil on pan; set dial at 350°F. and heat for 3 minutes. Pour off oil and wipe with paper towel. No additional seasoning is required before next use.

Directions for use: Preheat pan at 350°F. Prepare batter; scantily fill given measure with batter. Pour into center of crêpe maker, lift and tilt pan quickly in circular motion. Turn after batter appears dull on top and edges have begun to brown (about 30 seconds). Remove with spatula to plate.

Advantage: Even heat distribution with accurate heat control. Manufacturer also recommends use for preparing omelets, frying small amounts of food and as heating unit for hors d'oeuvres.

1

How to Cook a Crêpe

For all its mystique, a crêpe is easy to make. Crêpe-making is a first lesson for many students of French cooking. The most important part of the lesson is practice. Don't expect your first crêpe to be perfect. In fact, the first crêpe off the pan is often discarded, or used as a sample for tasting, by even the best of cooks.

Basic Directions for Mixing Crêpes

The simplest and most universal technique for mixing crêpes is to combine ingredients in a pitcher, quart-measure, or bowl, and beat with a whisk, rotary beater, mixing fork, or a wooden mixing spoon. You can also beat the batter in an electric mixer, or whirl it quickly in a blender, for very smooth batter which can be used without a waiting period. Crêpe batters are really simple to mix, and require no special skill. Combine ingredients in the order in which they are listed in each recipe.

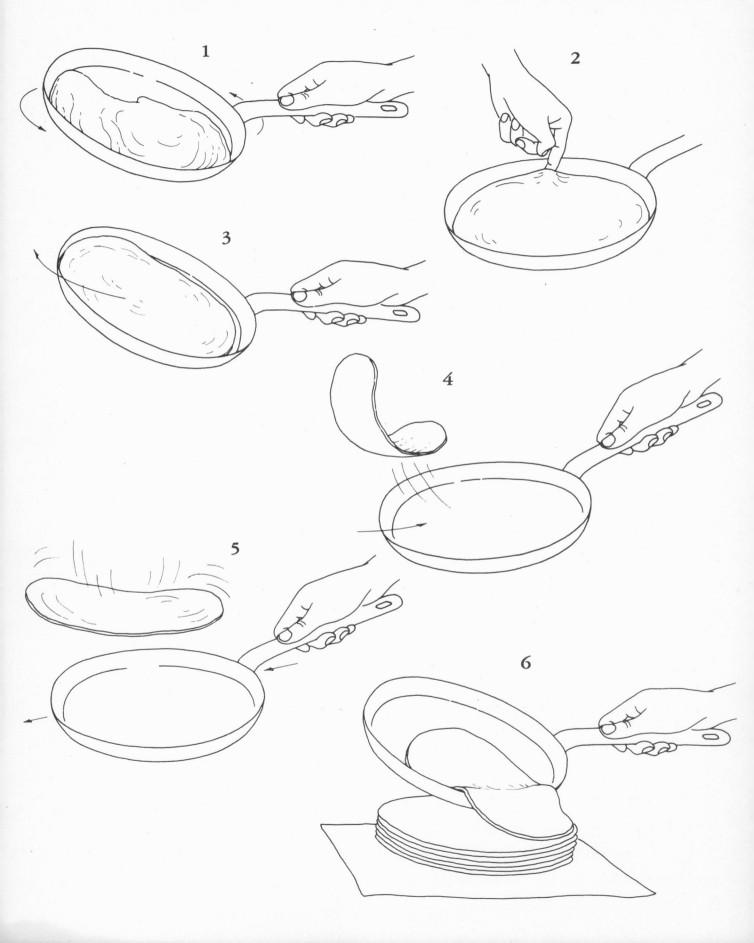

Basic Directions for Cooking Crêpes— Conventional Pans

1. Preheat the well-seasoned pan; grease lightly. Have crêpe batter as thick as heavy cream, in a pitcher or pour-measure. Stir well; if batter has thickened on standing, stir in a *little* water or milk, or an extra egg.

2. Holding the handle of the pan with one hand, pour about 2 tablespoons of batter into the center of the heated pan.

3. Tilt and turn the pan rapidly to spread the batter evenly over the bottom. Set directly over heat.

4. Let cook about half a minute, until surface is set and bottom dry enough to come away from the pan with ease, and browned to taste. Give the pan a shake or rap it against the range edge to loosen crêpe from the bottom; or loosen the crêpe with your fingers. Holding the pan in one hand, off the heat, thrust the pan forward and upward with a short, quick motion of the wrist, pull it back rapidly to flip the crêpe in the air, then move the pan quickly forward to catch the crêpe as it comes down, reversed. This technique takes a little practice, but once learned it is easy to do or to pick up again after a practice flip or two. Use your fingers rather than a spatula to turn the crêpe, being careful not to tear the crêpe.

5. Cook on second side 15 to 20 seconds longer. This second side browns less evenly, and is generally rolled inside the crêpe.

6. Slide finished crêpes from pan and stack on a flat paper-lined surface or a tray large enough to hold them without curling. Repeat, wiping the pan with a fat-saturated paper towel before cooking each crêpe. To use two pans at a time, begin the second a minute after the first.

Basic Directions for Cooking Crêpes— Upside-Down Pans

An awkward hand at spreading crêpes first devised the idea of dipping the *outside* bottom of a pan into the batter to coat it, then putting the pan upside down over the heat to cook the crêpe. Now many cooks find that this method is easier, and that it produces crêpes of more uniform size.

Choose a heavy 6-inch iron frying pan or omelet pan, or use one of the upside-down crêpe makers (pages 12-15)—or use both to make crêpes faster, and compare the results for yourself. Have the batter ready in an 8- or 9-inch pie plate or shallow dinner plate.

1. Place the pan upside down over a burner, at fairly high heat, until it is hot enough so that a drop of water splatters when it hits the pan. Remove from heat, rub the bottom of the pan with a thin coating of oil (some makers say oil the inside too, though this seems to produce more smoke than effective results).

2. Dip the bottom of the pan in the batter, let it just sizzle, and lift out immediately.

3. The bottom of the pan should be coated with a thin layer of batter. If it isn't, repeat; or patch the crêpe by filling any bare spot with a little batter.

4. Place the pan upside down over heat and cook until the bottom of crêpe begins to brown— less than a minute. Loosen edges with spatula, shake pan to release the crêpe.

5. Turn crêpe and cook for 10 seconds or so on the second side, unless you are using a pan curved and designed to brown both sides simultaneously.

Note: If batter falls back into the pie plate after dipping, the pan may be too hot or too well oiled. Use just a thin film of oil and cool the pan slightly between crêpes. If some batter falls back, strain out lumpy portions and use the rest.

Crêpes cooked on the bottom of the pan are slightly thinner and more elastic, but less tender, than those cooked in the pan.

Storing Crêpes

Store cooled crêpes to be refrigerated or frozen for later use with separators of squares of waxed paper. The paper should be slightly larger than the crêpes, for easy peel-off.

To keep crêpes for up to three days: Cover, store in the refrigerator.

To freeze for longer storage: Brown crêpes on both sides. (Do not freeze crêpes browned only

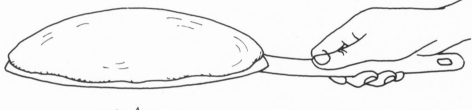

on one side, as these will tear when defrosted.) Cool thoroughly. Stack the number you are likely to use at one time, with squares of waxed paper between crêpes. Enclose each stack completely in heavy foil, double-folding the edges. To thaw for filling and rolling: place the package in a covered dish in a slow oven (300°F.) about 10 minutes, until warm enough to separate and roll; or remove the foil and heat about 1 minute in microwave oven.

Reheating Crêpes

To reheat a quantity of filled crêpes, place side by side, seam down, in a well-buttered casserole. Lace top with melted butter, or with sauce or sour cream, and heat in a moderately hot oven (375°F.) about 20 to 25 minutes. To reheat folded crêpes in sauce, as for Crêpes Suzette, prepare sauce in a shallow, flat pan. When sauce is bubbling, fold crêpes into the pan, lacing well with sauce, flame if desired, and serve as the flames die down.

Tips and Gadgets to Help in Making Crêpes

A one quart cup is handy for measuring, mixing, storing, and pouring the crêpe batter. A 2-quart measure pitcher is now designed for mixing batter, and is a handy size for refrigerator storage. A flat wooden crêpe "hoe" helps spread the batter evenly on a flat-surfaced pan, particularly a larger surface, such as the butane-heated plate. The flat side of a rubber spatula also does well.

A coffee measure (2 tablespoons) is handy for uniform distribution of batter in a pan for smaller (6-inch) crêpes. For larger crêpes in a larger pan, use a demi-tasse cup, or a ¼ cup measure.

Serving Tips

For easy service, set out crêpes and an assortment of fillings, let guests fill and roll their own crêpes to taste. If you have a microwave oven, it is ideal for reheating crêpes, especially for crêpes with such quick-cook fillings as sliced apples and cinnamon, or Raclette or Gruyère cheese, which melt deliciously in a minute. To keep crêpes warm, place in covered dish and put in slow oven (200°F.)

The Shape of Crêpes

Roll: Put the filling on the lower half of the crêpe, fold the bottom quarter over the filling. Roll once or twice more. Use for dessert and main-dish crêpes.

Envelopes: Put the filling on the center of the crêpe. Fold in one side then the other to par-tially cover the filling. Fold the bottom up and the top down to shape a secure envelope. Use for Blintzes, Spring Rolls, and other crêpes which are fried after filling.

Cigars: Spread filling evenly on crêpes, roll up tightly, cigar fashion. Use for snacks or sweets to eat out of hand.

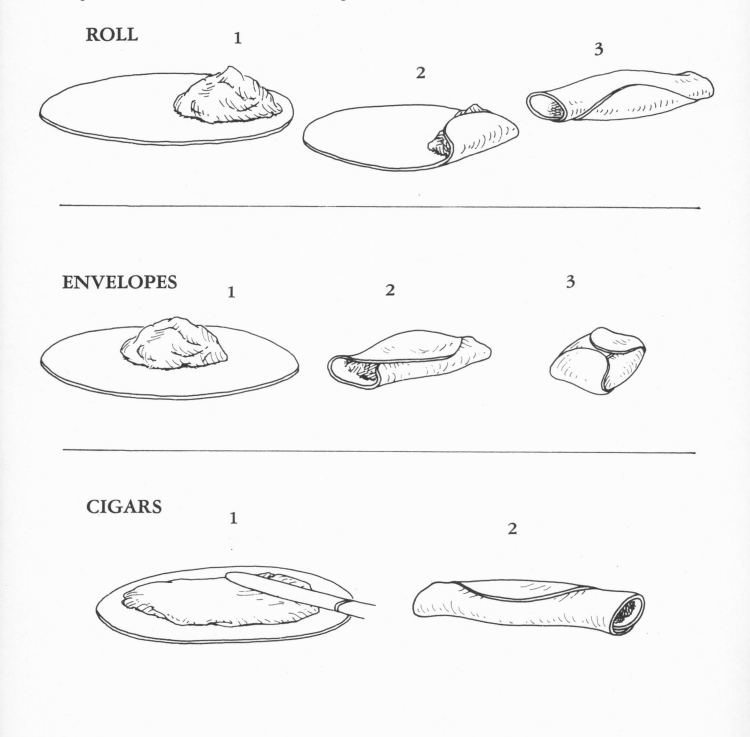

ROLL   1   3

                                              2

ENVELOPES   1   2   3

CIGARS   1   2

Appetizers: Cut cigar shapes into pieces or cut bite-sized triangles with a sharp knife.

Triangles: Put the filling in the top right-hand quarter of the crêpes. Fold the bottom half over the filling, fold the left quarter over the right quarter to shape a triangle.

APPETIZERS

1

2

TRIANGLES

1

2

3

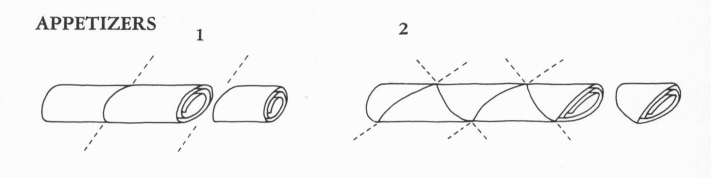

Pockets: Fold the crêpe into a triangle, as on page 23. Lift the top flap, spoon filling into the pocket.

Cone: Cut crêpes in half. Spread filling in the center of the half crêpe, shape a pointed cone by folding one side over the other.

Fold: Put the filling in the center of the crêpes, fold first one side then the other over the filling. Use when you want filling to show at ends of crêpe.

POCKETS

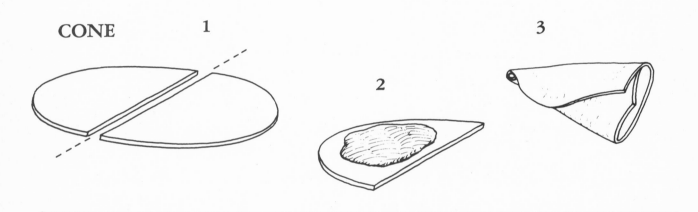

CONE

FOLD

A Variety of Crêpe Batters

Almost every country in the world has its favorite crêpes, made characteristically with white flour, rice flour, or buckwheat, with many eggs or few eggs, with milk or with water. These crêpes are filled with sweet or with savory mixtures and served as snack, main dish, or dessert.

We present here specific recipes for twenty-four of these crêpes of all nations. Fillings devised especially for each crêpe are suggested in the chapters which follow—with the understanding that mix-and-match pairing of fillings and crêpes is one of the joys of crêpe making.

Classic French Crêpes or Dessert Crêpes

2 eggs	1 cup flour
2 egg yolks	½ teaspoon salt
1¼ cups milk	2 tablespoons butter

Beat eggs and egg yolks with milk, using whisk, rotary beater, or fork. Add flour and salt, beat smooth. Batter should be of the consistency of heavy cream. Heat butter in small pan, spoon off foam (see clarified butter, page 9), pour clear yellow portion into batter. Let stand at least 30 minutes. Cook as in Basic Directions (page 17). Makes 12 to 16 crêpes.

Dessert Crêpes

Prepare as above, adding 2 tablespoons sugar to flour and salt, and beating in 2 tablespoons brandy, or orange-flavored liqueur for fruited crêpes; crème de cacao for chocolate fillings; kirsch for berry fillings—or to your taste.

Blender Crêpes

1 cup milk or half-and-half	½ teaspoon salt
4 eggs	1 tablespoon butter
1 cup flour	

Combine ingredients except butter in blender container, whirl until just combined. Melt butter in crêpe pan, pour into batter. Let batter stand at least 30 minutes, if convenient. Cook as in Basic Directions (page 17). Makes 12 to 16 crêpes.

Economy Crêpes

1 whole egg	1 cup flour
1 cup water	½ teaspoon salt
¼ cup instant nonfat milk solids	

Beat egg with water. Add milk solids, flour, and salt, beat until smooth. Let stand at least 30 minutes. Cook as in Basic Directions (page 17). Makes 12 to 16 crêpes.

Quick Crêpes

3 eggs	½ cup prepared pancake mix
½ cup milk	

Beat eggs with milk, add pancake mix, beat smooth. Cook as in Basic Directions (page 17). Makes 12 to 16 crêpes.

French Fines Herbes Crêpes

2 eggs	1 teaspoon fresh chopped tarragon
2 egg yolks	1 teaspoon fresh chopped chervil or chives
1 cup milk	2 tablespoons butter
1¼ cups flour	
½ teaspoon salt	
1 teaspoon fresh chopped parsley	

Beat eggs and egg yolks with milk. Add flour and salt, beat smooth. Stir in herbs until blended. Batter should be of the consistency of heavy cream. Melt butter in crêpe pan, pour into batter. Let stand at least 30 minutes. Cook as in Basic Directions (page 17). Makes 12 to 16 crêpes.

French Almond Crêpes

2 eggs	¼ cup toasted, pulverized almonds
2 egg yolks	¼ teaspoon salt
1 cup milk	2 tablespoons butter
2 tablespoons brandy	
¾ cup flour	

Beat eggs and egg yolks with milk and brandy. Add flour, almonds, and salt, beat smooth. Batter should be consistency of heavy cream. Melt butter in crêpe pan, pour into batter. Let stand at least 30 minutes. Cook as in Basic Directions (page 17). Makes 12 to 16 crêpes.

French Chocolate Crêpes

2 eggs	¾ cup flour
2 egg yolks	3 tablespoons cocoa powder
1¼ cups milk	½ teaspoon salt
2 tablespoons crème de cacao or chocolate liqueur	2 tablespoons butter

Beat eggs and egg yolks with milk and liqueur. Add flour, cocoa powder, and salt, beat smooth. Batter should be consistency of heavy cream. Melt butter in crêpe pan, pour into batter. Let stand at least 30 minutes. Cook as in Basic Directions (page 17). Makes 12 to 16 crêpes.

Chinese Crêpes

2 eggs	2 tablespoons cornstarch
2 cups water	½ teaspoon salt
1 cup flour	

Beat eggs lightly, add water, blend. Add flour mixed with cornstarch and salt to make a very thin batter. Let stand at least 30 minutes. Cook as in Basic Directions (page 17) on only one side. Makes 20 or more crêpes for Chinese dishes or "wrappers" for Chinese eggrolls and other oriental specialties.

Frittatine (Italian Crêpes)

1 egg	2 tablespoons olive oil
1 egg yolk	1 cup flour
½ cup milk	½ teaspoon salt
½ cup water	

Beat egg and yolk with milk and water, add oil. Beat in flour and salt, beat until smooth. Let stand at least 30 minutes. Cook as in Basic Directions (page 17). Makes 12 to 16 crêpes for cannelloni and other main-course crêpe dishes.

Blintzes

2 eggs	½ teaspoon salt
1½ cups milk	2 tablespoons butter
1 cup flour	

Beat eggs with milk, add flour and salt, beat smooth. Melt butter in crêpe pan, pour into batter, blend. Let stand at least 30 minutes. Cook in buttery pan on one side only until lightly browned. Turn out on paper or toweling, browned side up. Makes 12 to 16 blintzes.

Palacsinta (Hungarian Crêpes)

2 eggs, separated	1 cup flour
¾ cup milk	½ teaspoon salt
¾ cup water	Optional: sugar, liqueur

Beat egg yolks with milk and water, add flour and salt, beat smooth. Let stand at least 30 minutes. Just before making crêpes, beat egg whites to rounded peaks and fold in. Cook as in Basic Directions (page 17). Makes about 20 crêpes.

For Sweet Palacsinta, add ¼ cup sugar, 2 tablespoons liqueur to batter before letting stand.

Plättar (Swedish Pancakes)

1 cup flour	3 eggs
2 tablespoons sugar	2½ cups milk
¼ teaspoon salt	Butter

Sift flour into bowl, add sugar and salt. Add eggs and milk gradually, stirring until well blended. Let stand 2 hours. Heat a partitioned Swedish Plättar pan or a crêpe pan and butter well. Beat batter again, pour by tablespoons into sections of pan and brown on both sides. Serve immediately with lingonberries. Makes about 50 small Plättar.

Blini (Russian Pancakes)

½ envelope active dry yeast	½ teaspoon salt
¼ cup water (75-90°)	3 eggs
1¼ cups milk (75-90°)	1 teaspoon sugar
⅔ cup buckwheat flour	1 tablespoon butter, melted
⅓ cup white flour	

Dissolve yeast in warm water, add half the milk and half the flour, beat well. Let rise in a warm place, covered, 2 hours. Beat in remaining flour and salt. Beat eggs with remaining milk and sugar, add to batter with melted butter. Beat well. Let rise, covered, about 1 hour. Add more milk, if necessary, to make batter thin as heavy cream. Make very small crêpes by carefully spooning batter by tablespoons, well apart, on a hot, greased griddle. Turn once to brown both sides. Makes about 25 blini.

Beer Crêpes

2 eggs	1 teaspoon salt
2 egg yolks	1 tablespoon sour cream
1 cup beer	1 tablespoon melted butter
1 cup flour	

Beat eggs and egg yolks. Add beer and flour, beat until smooth. Beat in salt, sour cream, and melted butter. Cook as in Basic Directions (page 17). Makes 14 to 18 crêpes.

Eggnog Crêpes

2½ cups leftover holiday eggnog	¼ teaspoon salt
	2 tablespoons butter
1 cup flour	

Beat eggnog with flour and salt until mixture is smooth. Melt butter in crêpe pan, pour into batter. Let stand at least 30 minutes. Cook as in Basic Directions (page 17). Makes 12 to 16 crêpes.

Tortilla Crêpes

3 eggs	½ cup masa* harina
1½ cups milk	½ cup flour
2 tablespoons vegetable oil	½ teaspoon salt

Beat eggs with milk and oil. Gradually add masa, flour, and salt, beat very smooth. Let stand an hour

*Masa is a very fine flour made from dehydrated corn treated with lime water. It is available at Mexican specialty stores.

or longer. Cook as in Basic Directions (page 17). Reheat and soften on griddle, in oven on greased sheet, or microwave before filling. Makes 12 to 16 tortillas.

Whole Wheat Crêpes

2 eggs	½ cup white flour
2 egg yolks	½ teaspoon salt
1½ cups milk	1 tablespoon melted butter
½ cup whole wheat flour	

Beat eggs and egg yolks with milk, add flours and salt, beat until smooth. Stir in melted butter. Let stand at least 30 minutes. Cook as in Basic Directions (page 17). Makes 12 to 16 crêpes.

Sourdough Crêpes

1 cup sourdough starter	2 egg yolks
2 cups warm water	1 teaspoon salt
2½ cups flour	1 tablespoon sugar
2 eggs	2 tablespoons oil

Combine starter, water, and flour. Stir well, let stand overnight in a warm place. Remove 1 cup of starter mixture and store in the refrigerator for future use. Add to the remaining batter: eggs, egg yolks, salt, sugar, and oil, beat well. Cook as in Basic Directions (page 17), turning once to brown both sides well. Makes 30 to 32 crêpes with subtle, distinctive sourdough flavor.

Tip: If you don't have a starter batter, the simplest way to begin one is with a package of dry sourdough mix. Return a cup of newly fermented batter to the bowl or jar in the refrigerator each time you use it.

Bran Crêpes

2 cups milk	½ teaspoon salt
¼ cup bran	2 teaspoons sugar
2 eggs, beaten	2 tablespoons melted butter
¾ cup flour	or oil

Pour milk over bran, let stand 10 minutes. Add eggs. Combine flour, salt, and sugar, add to bran mixture, blending well. Stir in butter. Cook as in Basic Directions (page 17). Makes 12 to 16 crêpes.

Soy Flour Crêpes

1 egg	1 teaspoon brown sugar
1½ cups milk	¼ teaspoon salt
¼ cup soy flour	1 tablespoon melted butter
¾ cup whole wheat flour	

Beat egg with milk. Combine and add flours, sugar, and salt, beat until smooth. Stir in melted butter. Cook as in Basic Directions (page 17). The mixture may thicken as it stands; add more milk as required, stirring well after addition. Makes 12 to 16 crêpes.

Buttermilk Crêpes

1 egg	½ teaspoon baking soda
1½ cups buttermilk	2 teaspoons sugar
1 cup flour	1 tablespoon melted butter
Pinch of salt	

Beat egg with buttermilk. Combine flour, salt, baking soda, and sugar, add to egg mixture, beat smooth. Stir in butter. Let stand at least 30 minutes. Cook as in Basic Directions (page 17). Makes 12 to 16 crêpes.

Yogurt Crêpes

Substitute 1 cup of yogurt and ½ cup of milk for the buttermilk in the recipe for Buttermilk Crêpes (above). Cook as in Basic Directions (page 17). Makes 12 to 16 crêpes.

Low-Cholesterol Crêpes

1¼ cups milk	¼ teaspoon salt
2 egg whites	2 tablespoons safflower,
½ cup rice flour	corn, or soybean oil
½ cup all-purpose flour	

Beat milk and egg whites, add flours and salt, beat until smooth. Stir in oil. Let stand at least 30 minutes. Cook as in Basic Directions (page 17). Makes 14 to 18 crêpes.

Crêpes for a Crowd

8 eggs	1 cup flour
½ quart milk	1½ teaspoons salt
½ quart water	½ cup butter, melted
1 cup cornstarch	

Beat eggs, milk, and water. Gradually beat in cornstarch, flour, and salt, beat smooth. Add butter, blend. Let stand at least 30 minutes. Cook as in Basic Directions (page 17). Makes 60 crêpes.

2
French Crêpes, Classic and Otherwise

Some food lore has it that the first French crêpes were made by a Flemish maiden welcoming a prince and his hungry entourage when they arrived unexpectedly for a meal. She added extra eggs to a plain pancake batter and served a quick but delectable repast . . . and they lived happily ever after.

Crêpes have come a long way since then, touched with the genius of chefs for such specialties as Crêpes Soufflées Rothschild and Crêpes Suzette. The marvel is that the same basic batter can turn out dishes of so varied flavor, and that many crêpe batters may be interchanged, to your taste and convenience.

Most frequently used for these specialties is the batter for Classic French Crêpes, page 25. Or use the Economy Crêpes, page 25, or Blender Crêpes, page 25, or Palacsinta, page 26, or even Whole Wheat Crêpes or Blini, pages 27 and 26. Dessert Crêpes, page 25, Classic French Crêpes sweetened and flavored with brandy, are the basis of many dessert specialties. Any of the white flour crêpes named are also suitable for the desserts described in this section.

Appetizer Crêpes

Crêpes aux Fruits de Mer
(Seafood Crêpes)

¼ cup butter	1 tablespoon grated Parmesan cheese
¼ cup flour	san cheese
2 cups milk	Salt, pepper
2 ounces Swiss cheese, grated (½ cup)	1 pound crab meat
	Slivered almonds (optional)

Make Classic French Crêpes (page 25), brown on both sides, keep warm. Melt butter; stir in flour, and cook for a moment. Gradually add milk and cook, stirring, until the sauce is thickened and smooth. Add grated cheese, stir to blend. Adjust seasoning with salt and pepper. Pick over crab meat and discard shells and membranes. Combine half the sauce with the crab meat. Divide crab meat onto hot crêpes, fold. Arrange on individual serving dishes. Cover with remaining sauce. Sprinkle top with slivered almonds, if desired. The crêpes may be arranged on a flameproof serving dish, covered with sauce, and placed under the broiler flame to brown lightly before serving. Fills 16 crêpes.

Crêpes aux Anchois
(Anchovy and Egg Crêpes)

6 hard-cooked eggs	Mayonnaise
6 ribs of celery	Paprika
8 anchovies	Pepper

Make Classic French Crêpes (page 25), brown on both sides, cut in half, keep warm. Chop eggs, mince celery finely. Wash anchovies, drain, mince finely. Blend ingredients, use enough mayonnaise to make a spreadable mixture. Spread mixture on crêpes, fold into triangles. Fills 12 to 16 crêpes.

Crêpes aux Crevettes l'Indienne
(Curried Shrimp Crêpes)

2 tablespoons butter	Pinch ground ginger
1 onion, chopped	Pinch salt
1½ tablespoons flour	Dash cayenne
¾ to 1 teaspoon curry powder (or more, to taste)	¾ pound peeled, deveined shrimp
½ cup applesauce	1 tablespoon lemon juice
½ cup beef or chicken bouillon	

Make Classic French Crêpes (page 25), brown on both sides, keep warm. Melt butter, sauté chopped onion until translucent. Stir in flour and curry powder, cook for a moment, stirring. Add applesauce and bouillon, stir well. Bring to a boil, stirring, season to taste with spices and cook over low heat, stirring often, until sauce is thickened and smooth.

Add shrimp, cook very briefly until just done, from 2 to 5 minutes, depending on size. Overcooking toughens shrimp and makes them mealy. Add lemon juice. Spoon shrimp and sauce onto crêpes, roll up, serve hot. Fills 12 to 16 crêpes.

Crêpes au Consommé
(Crêpe Noodles for Consommé)

Leftover crêpes, or crêpes specially prepared for this purpose, may be sliced into thin, noodlelike strips and used to garnish consommés and other soups.

Main Dish Crêpes

Crêpes Soufflées à l'Homard
(Lobster Soufflé Crêpes)

1 cup cooked lobster meat, diced	½ teaspoon salt
¼ cup brandy (optional)	⅛ teaspoon pepper
4 tablespoons butter	Cayenne, nutmeg
3 tablespoons flour	1 teaspoon lemon juice
¾ cup milk	4 egg yolks
	5 egg whites

Make large Classic French Crêpes (page 25), browning only one side. (Crêpes may be made ahead for this dish.) Sprinkle lobster with brandy, let stand. Melt butter, stir in flour, and cook for a minute. Gradually add milk and cook, stirring, until the sauce is thickened and smooth. Season to taste, add lemon juice. Beat 4 egg yolks well, combine with sauce. Add lobster brandy. Beat 5 egg whites until they stand in stiff peaks, fold in gently. Fold the crêpes into quarters, browned side in. Lift the top flap and fill the cone with soufflé mixture. Arrange on buttered baking dish, bake in a hot oven (425°F.) 10 minutes or longer, until the soufflé mixture sets and browns around edges. Makes about 8 main dish crêpes.

Crêpes au Saucisse
(Sausage Crêpes)

½ pound sausage meat	2 green peppers, slivered

Make Classic French Crêpes (page 25). Keep warm. Cook sausage meat in a skillet, stirring occasionally to separate pieces. Drain off excess fat. Add peppers and stir over heat for a minute. Spoon mixture onto crêpes, roll up, serve at once. Fills about 8 crêpes.

Crêpes au Jambon
(Ham Crêpes)

2 tablespoons butter	Salt, pepper
¼ cup milk	Thin slices ham
¼ pound Gruyère cheese, grated	

Make large Classic French Crêpes (page 25). Melt butter, add milk, heat, add cheese, stir to blend. Add seasonings to taste. Spread mixture on crêpes, cover with a slice of ham, roll up. Arrange on buttered shallow baking dish, bake in a moderate oven (350°F.) about 15 minutes. Fills about 8 crêpes.

Gâteau de Crêpes aux Épinards
(Layered Spinach Crêpes)

2 packages frozen chopped spinach (about 2 cups cooked)	1 teaspoon sugar
	Nutmeg, salt, pepper
1 tablespoon butter	1 cup Mornay Sauce
1 tablespoon flour	¼ cup grated Swiss cheese
3 tablespoons half-and-half or cream	

Prepare large Classic French Crêpes (page 25). Cook spinach as directed, drain thoroughly. Melt butter, add flour, and stir for a moment. Add half-and-half, cook and stir until smooth. Add drained spinach, sugar, nutmeg, salt, and pepper to taste. Stack the crêpes on a buttered baking dish with layers of the spinach mixture between them. Cover with Mornay Sauce, sprinkle with grated cheese. Bake in a hot oven (400°F.) until the cheese melts and the stack is piping hot, 10 to 15 minutes. Serves 6 to 8.

Crêpes Ile de France
(Crêpes with Ham and Mushrooms)

¼ pound thinly sliced ham	Salt, pepper
½ pound fresh mushrooms, chopped	2 tablespoons flour
	2 cups milk
4 tablespoons butter	¼ cup grated Swiss cheese

Make Classic French Crêpes (page 25), turning once to brown both sides. Cover each with thinly sliced ham. Cook mushrooms in 2 tablespoons butter, season with salt and pepper to taste. Divide onto crêpes, roll up, arrange on a buttered shallow baking dish. Melt remaining butter, add flour, and cook for a moment, stirring. Add milk and cook, stirring constantly, until the sauce is thickened and smooth. Adjust seasonings with salt and pepper. Pour the sauce over the crêpes. Sprinkle with cheese, bake in a moderate oven (350°F.) about 15 minutes until bubbling hot and browned. Fills about 8 crêpes.

Crêpes Paysanne
(Farmer's Crêpes)

3 tablespoons butter	Salt, pepper
1 cup cooked potatoes, diced	4 eggs
1 large onion, chopped	2 tablespoons milk

Make Classic French Crêpes (page 25), keep warm. Melt butter in a skillet, add potatoes and onion, cook until golden. Sprinkle with salt and pepper to taste. Beat eggs with milk, season to taste, quickly stir into skillet. Spoon creamy mixture onto crêpes, fold in half, serve at once. Fills 12 crêpes.

Crêpes au Ratatouille
(Crêpes with Vegetable Stew)

2 tablespoons oil	½ cup diced eggplant
1 small onion, diced	1 tomato, peeled, seeded, chopped
½ green pepper, diced	
1 clove garlic, minced	Basil, salt, pepper
½ cup diced zucchini	

Make Classic French Crêpes (page 25), keep warm. Heat oil, cook onion, green pepper, and garlic until onion is golden. Add remaining ingredients, simmer gently until mixture is thick, about 10 minutes. Spoon onto crêpes, roll up, serve hot.

Crêpes de Provence
(Mushrooms in Tomato Sauce Crêpes)

1 pound mushrooms, washed and sliced	Salt, freshly ground black pepper
¼ cup butter	1 cup Tomato Sauce (below)
½ cup black olives, drained, pitted, and sliced	

Reserve crêpes. Simmer mushrooms in butter for 5 minutes, covered. Stir in olives, salt, and pepper to taste, continue cooking until mushrooms are tender. Remove from heat, add ¼ cup Tomato Sauce (below). Spoon mushroom mixture onto each crêpe and roll up. Arrange seam side down in a buttered baking dish and cover with remaining sauce. Bake in a moderate oven (375°F.) for 30 minutes. Fills about 8 crêpes.

Tomato Sauce

1 small onion, finely chopped	1 bay leaf
1 rib celery, finely chopped	⅛ teaspoon basil
4 tablespoons olive oil	¼ teaspoon oregano
¼ cup chopped parsley	2 pounds ripe tomatoes, peeled, seeded, and coarsely chopped
3 cloves garlic, minced	
Salt, freshly ground black pepper to taste	

In a heavy-bottomed saucepan, sauté onions and celery in hot oil, stirring frequently, until onions are translucent. Stir in remaining ingredients and simmer, stirring occasionally, for 45 minutes or until the consistency of a thick puree. Remove from heat, force through a food mill or sieve. Makes about 2½ cups.

Crêpes Niçoise
(Fish Salad Crêpes)

½ pound cut green beans, crisply cooked	⅔ cup olive oil
1 cup diced boiled potatoes	1 egg yolk
1 can (7 ounces) tuna	2 tablespoons wine vinegar
2 hard-cooked eggs, cut into small wedges	2 teaspoons chopped parsley
½ cup small pitted black olives	½ teaspoon salt
	½ teaspoon pepper
	½ teaspoon dry mustard
1 can (2 ounces) anchovy fillets, drained	1½ cups tomato sauce (optional)

Prepare Classic French Crêpes (page 25), keep warm. Combine beans, potatoes, tuna, egg wedges, and olives in bowl. Add 3 tablespoons of the oil, toss to coat. In bowl or blender, beat egg yolk with vinegar and seasonings, beat in remaining oil very gradually until thickened. Pour sauce over mixture in bowl and toss lightly to combine. Spoon onto crêpes, fold over and serve. Top with hot tomato sauce, if desired. Makes about 16 crêpes.

Desserts

Crêpes Suzette
(Crêpes with Blazing Orange Sauce)

¼ cup butter	¼ cup orange-flavored liqueur
8 cubes sugar	
1 navel orange	¼ cup brandy
½ lemon	

Make Classic French Crêpes (page 25), fold into quarters. These may be prepared in advance. Melt butter in a heavy pan. (Do this at the table for dramatic effect.) Rub sugar cubes against orange rind, then drop into butter, stir over heat until sugar melts. Squeeze juice from orange and lemon and add. Grate rind and add, bring to a boil. Stir in orange liqueur, heat until sauce is blended. Turn the folded crêpes in the sauce to heat. Warm brandy in a ladle, ignite it, and pour flaming over the crêpes. Baste crêpes with the sauce until the flames die. Makes 6 to 8 servings.

Tropical French Crêpes Suzette

Prepare Classic French Crêpes (page 25), keep warm. Spoon on filling of guava paste or jelly and roll up. Dust with cinnamon and confectioners' sugar. Heat ¼ cup rum, ignite and pour blazing over crêpes at the dinner table for a dramatic effect.

Crêpes Suzette aux Petites
(Crêpes Suzette for Children)

⅓ cup butter	1 tablespoon lemon juice
½ cup sugar	1 tablespoon grated orange peel
½ cup orange juice	

Prepare Classic French Crêpes (page 25), fold prepared crêpes into quarters. Melt butter in a heavy pan, add sugar, stir until sugar melts. Add remaining ingredients, heat. Add crêpes and heat, turning once. Makes 12 to 16 crêpes.

Crêpes Normande
(Apple Crêpes)

3 cups thinly sliced apples	¼ cup sugar, or to taste
¼ cup butter	

Make Classic French Crêpes (page 25), keep warm. Cook apple slices gently in butter, a few at a time. They should retain their shape. Sprinkle very lightly with sugar to taste. Spoon onto cooked crêpes, roll up. Arrange the filled crêpes on a buttered shallow baking dish, dust with more sugar and place under the broiler for a moment until sugar is lightly glazed. Or, heat filled crêpes in microwave oven, on serving plate. Makes 16 to 20 crêpes.

Crêpes Anjou
(Crêpes with Pears)

2 pears	1 teaspoon Cognac
2 tablespoons orange juice	1 cup sugar
2 tablespoons lemon juice	2 tablespoons butter
1 teaspoon vanilla	½ cup brandy
1 teaspoon orange-flavored liqueur	

Prepare Classic French Crêpes (page 25) in advance. Peel, core, and cut pears lengthwise into 6 wedges. Combine orange juice, lemon juice, vanilla, liqueur, Cognac, and sugar, boil to make a light syrup. Add pear sections and simmer for a few minutes. Put 1 pear wedge and a little syrup on each crêpe, fold up. At the table, melt butter in a chafing dish, add the crêpes, pour the remaining syrup over them. Warm the brandy, ignite it, and pour flaming over the crêpes. Serve at once. Makes 12 crêpes.

Crêpes aux Confitures
(Jam Crêpes)

Make Classic French Crêpes (page 25). Spread thinly with favorite jam or preserves, roll up, dust with powdered sugar, serve at once.

Caramelized Jam Crêpes

Sprinkle Jam Crêpes (above) thickly with confectioners' sugar and arrange on a buttered shallow bak-

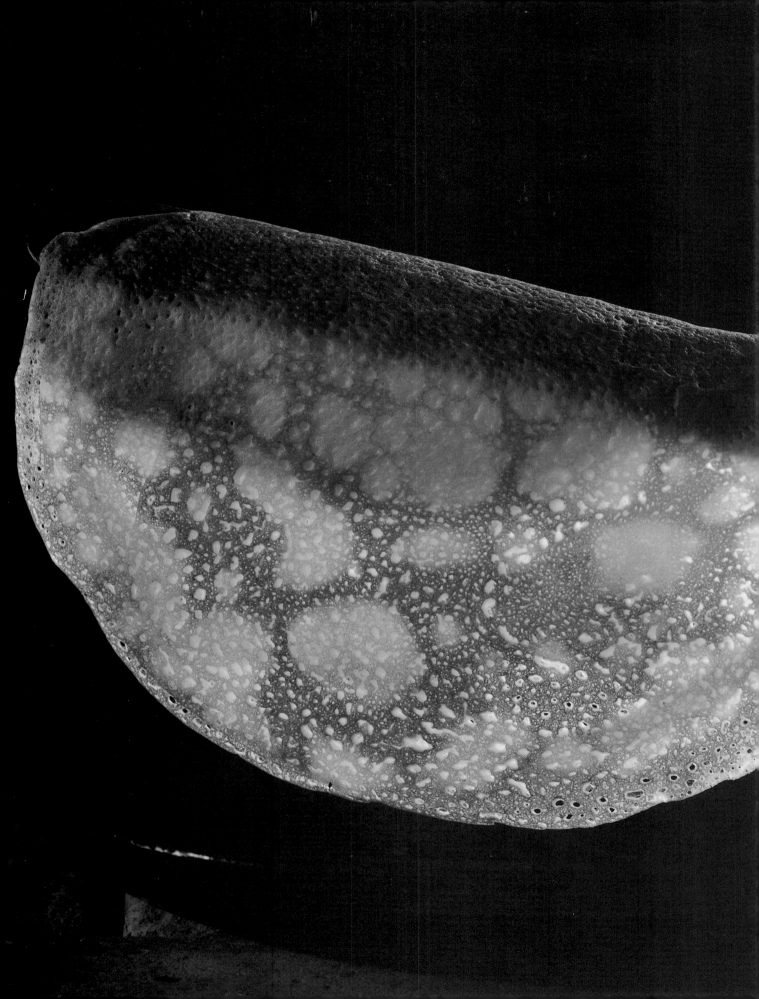

Guacamole for Tortillas (*page 88*)

Smoked Salmon Crêpes (*page 36*)

Lobster Soufflé Crêpes (*page 30*)

Beef Stroganoff for Blini (*page 79*)

Fish in Sharp Sauce Palacsinta *(page 72)*

Preparing Fish in Sharp Sauce Palacsinta

Gâteau de Crêpes aux Epinards *(page 31)*

Veal Goulash Palacsinta (*page 72*)

Preparing Crêpe
Sandwiches
Monte Cristo

Crêpe Sandwiches Monte Cristo (*page 50*)

Quick Shrimp Marinara Crêpes *(page 65)*

Sweet and Pungent Pork Crêpes (*page 60*)

ing dish. Bake in a very hot oven (450°F.) for a few minutes to caramelize the sugar.

Crêpes Pralinées
(Praline Crêpes)

6 tablespoons butter	**3 tablespoons praline**
¼ cup superfine sugar	**powder (below)**
	Rum

Make Classic French Crêpes (page 25), keep warm. Cream butter with sugar, add praline powder and a little rum to taste. Spread the mixture on crêpes, roll tightly, cigar fashion, and serve at once. Fills 16 to 18 crêpes.

Praline Powder

¼ pound almonds, with	**½ cup sugar**
skins (1 cup)	

Heat nuts and sugar in a heavy pan over low heat until sugar begins to melt. Stir and continue cooking until sugar is a rich, caramel brown. Turn out on an oiled slab or plate to cool and harden. Break the praline into small pieces and use the electric blender to pulverize pieces. Or, put the pieces in a brown paper bag and crush with a wooden rolling pin. Makes about 1 cup powder, useful as a flavoring for varied dessert crêpes. Keeps well in an airtight tin.

Gâteau aux Crêpes Meringuées
(Meringue Crêpe Cake)

2 egg whites	**6 ounces semisweet**
½ teaspoon lemon juice	**chocolate, grated**
¼ cup sugar	

Prepare Classic French Crêpes (page 25). Beat egg whites foamy, add lemon juice, beat until soft peaks form when the beater is withdrawn. Gradually beat in sugar, continue to beat until stiff peaks form. Stack the crêpes, sprinkling each with grated chocolate. Top the "layer cake" thus formed with swirls of meringue. Bake in a hot oven (450°F.) until the tips of the meringue are richly golden. Serves 8 to 10.

Tip: Any dessert crêpe, filled with fruit or with cream and rolled up, or simply covered with sauce, may be topped with meringue and baked.

Crêpes Chartreuse
(Chartreuse Liqueur Crêpes)

½ cup butter	**3 tablespoons green Char-**
½ cup confectioners' sugar	**treuse**

Make Classic French Crêpes (page 25), keep warm. Cream butter with sugar, add Chartreuse. Spread on hot crêpes, fold into quarters. Serve dusted with more confectioners' sugar if desired. Fills 16 to 20 crêpes.

Note: Other liqueurs may be used in the same way.

Crêpes Frangipane
(Almond Cream Crêpes)

3 egg yolks	**⅓ cup finely chopped**
½ cup sugar	**almonds**
⅓ cup flour	**¼ teaspoon almond extract**
1½ cups hot milk	**½ teaspoon vanilla extract**
2 tablespoons butter	**Grated semisweet chocolate**

Make Classic French Crêpes (page 25), keep warm. Beat egg yolks in a saucepan, off the heat. Beat in sugar and flour. Gradually add hot milk. Cook over low heat, stirring, until the mixture is smooth and thickened. Add butter, nuts, and flavoring. Transfer to a bowl, cool before filling crêpes. Roll crêpes, sprinkle with grated semisweet chocolate, if desired. Fills 16 to 20 crêpes.

Crêpes Soufflées Rothschild
(Soufflé Crêpes with Candied Fruits)

2 tablespoons butter	**3 tablespoons finely chopped**
2 tablespoons flour	**candied fruit**
¾ cup milk	**2 eggs, separated**
Pinch salt	**3 tablespoons sugar**
1 tablespoon orange liqueur	

Prepare Classic French Crêpes (page 25) in advance. Melt butter, stir in flour, and cook for a minute. Gradually add milk. Add salt and cook, stirring, until the sauce is thick and smooth. Add liqueur and candied fruit. Beat in egg yolks one at a time. Beat egg whites foamy, gradually add sugar, beat stiff. Fold ¼ the beaten egg whites into the hot mixture, mixing thoroughly. Fold in remaining egg whites gently. Fold the crêpes into quarters, fill top flap with mixture. Bake on a buttered baking dish, hot oven (425°F.) about 10 minutes until the soufflé mixture is puffed. Dust with confectioners' sugar, serve at once. Makes 16 crêpes.

Creme Fraîche à l'Américaine

½ cup heavy cream	**½ cup yogurt**

Whip cream until it just holds its shape. Fold in yogurt, chill. Serve as a topping with dessert crêpes.

3

Blender Crêpes

These fillings are designed particularly for the Blender Crêpes batter (page 25), although that batter can also be used for almost any other filling in the book. The blender makes a smooth crêpe, which needs less standing time because the blades cut liquid and egg into the flour more thoroughly, speeding absorption. Many of these fillings may also be combined in a blender. All are quick to stir up, contemporary in mood, and delectable in flavor, whether for appetizer, main dish, or dessert.

Appetizer Crêpes

Blue Cheese Crêpes

4 ounces blue cheese (1 cup crumbled)	1 teaspoon Worcestershire sauce
½ pound (1 cup) small-curd cottage cheese	Beer

Make Blender Crêpes (page 25). Mash blue cheese with cottage cheese to make a smooth mixture. (Or, whirl in blender until smooth.) Season with Worcestershire sauce, add enough beer to make a spreadable mixture. Spread on reheated or cool crêpes, roll up cigar fashion. Fills 16 crêpes.

Shrimp Butter Crêpes

½ cup butter	1 cup cooked shrimp
2 tablespoons hot lemon juice	Salt, pepper, cayenne

Prepare Blender Crêpes (page 25). Combine butter with lemon juice in blender, whirl until smooth. Add shrimp, whirl to chop coarsely. Add seasonings to taste. Spread on crêpes, roll up. Makes about 8 crêpes.

Crêpes aux Tomates Provencales

1 slice bread	2 tablespoons chopped parsley
2 tomatoes	Salt, pepper
1 tablespoon oil	
½ teaspoon garlic powder	

Make Blender Crêpes (page 25) while tomato mixture (see below) is cooking. Tear bread in pieces, whirl in blender to make crumbs. Peel and seed tomatoes, chop coarsely. Heat oil in a saucepan, add tomatoes, bread crumbs, garlic powder. Cook, covered, until tomatoes are soft. Add parsley and salt and pepper to taste. Spoon onto hot crêpes, roll, serve at once. Fills 4 crêpes.

Clam and Sour Cream Crêpes

1 can (7 ounces) minced clams, drained	1 cup sour cream
	Salt, pepper, cayenne

Make Blender Crêpes (page 25). Drain clams well, mix with sour cream, season to taste. Or, whirl clams and sour cream in blender to make smooth mixture. Spoon onto warm or cooled crêpes, roll up. Fills 12 crêpes.

Smoked Salmon Crêpes

4 ounces smoked salmon	1 teaspoon lemon juice
½ pound cream cheese	

Make Blender Crêpes (page 25), keep warm. Mash cut-up salmon and cream cheese with lemon juice. Beat until smooth. Spread thinly on warm crêpes, roll up cigar fashion. Fills 20 crêpes.

Crab Crêpes

2 tablespoons butter	1 can (8 ounces) crabmeat
2 tablespoons flour	3 tablespoons sherry
1 cup milk	Salt, pepper
1 egg	
¼ cup grated Swiss cheese (1 ounce)	

Prepare Blender Crêpes (page 25) in advance, as convenient. Melt butter, stir in flour, cook for a minute, stirring. Add all but about 2 tablespoons milk and continue to cook, stirring, until the sauce is thickened and smooth. Beat egg with remaining milk, add to sauce. Add cheese. Pick over crabmeat, discarding shells and membranes. Heat crabmeat in sherry, boil rapidly for a minute until mixture is almost dry. Add to ¾ of the prepared sauce, adjust seasoning with salt and pepper. Fill crêpes, roll up. Arrange on a buttered baking dish, cover with a ribbon of reserved sauce, bake in a hot oven (400°F.) until sauce browns and crêpes are piping hot, about 15 minutes. Makes 12 servings.

Main Dish Crêpes

Salmon Crêpes

1 tablespoon minced onion	⅓ cup mayonnaise
2 tablespoons minced celery	Salt, pepper
1 tablespoon minced parsley	3 tablespoons melted butter
1 can (7 ounces) salmon	

Prepare Blender Crêpes (page 25) in advance. Combine mixed vegetables with salmon and mayonnaise, add salt and pepper to season well. Spoon onto crêpes, roll up, arrange side by side on a buttered baking dish. Drizzle with melted butter, bake in a hot oven (400°F.) about 15 minutes until crêpes are piping hot. Fills 6 crêpes.

Chicken and Apple Crêpes

1 cup cubed cooked chicken	¼ cup mayonnaise
¼ cup diced apple	Salt, pepper
2 tablespoons toasted slivered almonds	

Prepare Blender Crêpes (page 25). Combine ingredients in blender, whirl to chop coarsely, spoon onto crêpes, roll up. Fills 6 to 8.

Tuna Crêpes

½ cup cream or half-and-half	3 slices white bread, broken
1 egg	1 can (about 7 ounces) tuna
2 sprigs parsley	Pepper, salt, cayenne
2 celery tops	1½ tablespoons butter

Make Blender Crêpes (page 25) in advance, if desired. Put cream, egg, parsley, celery, and bread into the blender container, whirl until smooth. Add tuna and seasonings to taste. Divide onto crêpes, roll up. Arrange on a shallow buttered baking dish, dot with butter. Bake in a moderate oven (350°F.) about 20 minutes, until crêpes and filling are piping hot. Makes 12 crêpes.

Deviled Ham Crêpes

½ cup mayonnaise	½ teaspoon dry mustard
1 tart apple, peeled, sliced	1 teaspoon drained horse-radish
1 green pepper, sliced	
1 cup coarsely cut cooked ham	Hot pepper sauce
	Salt, pepper

Make Blender Crêpes (page 25), keep warm. Combine mayonnaise, apple, and green pepper in blender. Whirl until smooth. Add ham, whirl until ham is finely chopped. Stir in mustard, horseradish, and seasonings to taste. Spoon onto warm crêpes, roll up. Fills 12 to 16 crêpes.

Asparagus and Deviled Ham Crêpes

Make Blender Crêpes (page 25), spread with deviled ham mixture, above. Add 1 or 2 hot cooked or canned asparagus spears to each crêpe, roll.

Dessert Crêpes

Coffee Mallow Crêpes

½ cup coffee, brewed double-strength	1 cup heavy cream
¼ pound marshmallows, cut up	

Cook coffee and marshmallows over low heat, stirring constantly, until marshmallows are dissolved. Whip cream until stiff, fold into the cooled coffee-marshmallow mixture. Chill thoroughly. Make Blender Crêpes (page 25) just before serving. Fill warm crêpes, roll up. Serve as is, or with a sprinkling of confectioners' sugar and a faint dusting of finest-ground coffee. Fills 12 crêpes.

Peanut Butter Crêpes

1 cup heavy cream	½ teaspoon vanilla extract
2 tablespoons sugar	2 tablespoons peanut butter

Prepare Blender Crêpes (page 25). Whip cream with sugar until stiff, add vanilla. Reserve ¼ the cream for topping, mix remainder with peanut butter. Spoon onto crêpes, roll up. Top with reserved whipped cream. Fills about 6.

Maple Butter Cream Crêpes

3 tablespoons maple syrup	Dash salt
½ cup softened butter	½ cup heavy cream
Few drops almond extract	

Prepare Blender Crêpes (page 25). Keep warm. Put syrup, butter, extract, and salt into blender container. Blend until smooth. Gradually add cream, blend just until thickened. Spread cream thinly on crêpes, roll up cigar fashion. Fills 6 to 8 crêpes.

Chocolate Mousse Crêpes

3 ounces semisweet chocolate pieces (½ cup)	¼ pound butter, in pieces
¼ cup warmed crème de cacao or milk	2 eggs, separated
	1 tablespoon confectioners' sugar

Prepare Blender Crêpes (page 25), let stand at room temperature. Put chocolate pieces and warm crème de cacao or milk into the blender container. Whirl to melt the chocolate. Add butter and egg yolks, whirl again. Beat egg whites stiff with sugar, fold in chocolate mixture. Cool. Spoon onto crêpes, roll or fold. Fills 8 crêpes.

Lemon Curd Crêpes

3 eggs	Pinch salt
¾ cup sugar	¼ cup butter
⅓ cup lemon juice, fresh or bottled	

Prepare Blender Crêpes (page 25). Beat eggs in a saucepan, off the heat, until light and frothy. Beat in sugar, lemon juice, and salt. Add butter. Cook over low heat, stirring constantly, until the butter is melted and the cream is smooth and thickened. Cool, stirring occasionally. Spoon onto warm or cool crêpes, roll up. Fills 6 to 8 crêpes.

Crêpes aux Bananes à la Crème
(Banana and Cream Crêpes)

1 large, ripe banana   2 tablespoons brown sugar
1 cup sour cream (8 ounces)

Prepare Blender Crêpes (page 25). Slice banana, add sour cream and sugar, turn to coat banana pieces. Spoon onto prepared warm or cooled crêpes, roll up. Fills 6 crêpes.

Cream Cheese Fluff

8 ounces cream cheese,   2 tablespoons sugar
   softened
5 tablespoons cream or sour
   cream

Make Blender Crêpes (page 25). Whip cream cheese in blender with cream and sugar. Spoon onto 8 warm or cooled crêpes, roll up.

Whipped Cottage Cheese Crêpes

1 cup (8 ounces) creamed   2 tablespoons confectioners'
   cottage cheese   sugar
¼ cup sour cream

Make Blender Crêpes (page 25). Whip cottage cheese in blender with cream and sugar. Spoon onto 12 warm or cooled crêpes. Roll up.

Tip: Serve with fresh fruit, or with favorite fruit sauces, or with:

Brandied Strawberries

1 pint strawberries   Sugar to taste
2 tablespoons cherry brandy

Wash and hull berries, slice. Sprinkle with brandy and sugar to taste, spoon over fresh cheese crêpes (above). Serves 12.

Crêpes aux Marrons
(Chestnut Crêpes)

1 pound chestnuts   1 cup heavy cream
½ cup sugar
2 tablespoons rum (or
   liqueur)

Prepare Blender Crêpes (page 25). Slit a cross on the flat side of each chestnut, bring to a boil in water to cover, cook 15 minutes. Remove the nuts, cool them until shells and skins can be conveniently re-moved. Cover again with water, boil until very tender. Puree nuts in the blender. Add sugar and rum, or your favorite liqueur, to flavor. Whip cream, reserve ¼ for topping, blend remainder with the chestnut puree. Spoon onto crêpes, fold up, top with whipped cream. Cream may be sweetened and flavored with liqueur to taste. Fills about 12 crêpes.

Fresh Applesauce Crêpes

4 apples   2 tablespoons sugar, to taste
2 cups cold water   Cinnamon sugar
3 tablespoons lemon juice

Prepare Blender Crêpes (page 25) in advance. Cut apples into quarters, discard cores, but do not peel. Cut into pieces and drop directly into cold water mixed with lemon juice to prevent discoloring. Put ¼ cup of the lemon-water mixture into the blender container, add ½ cup apples at a time and whirl until smooth. Repeat until all apples are used. Add sugar to taste, blend to dissolve. Spoon onto crêpes, roll up. Arrange on a buttered baking dish, sprinkle with cinnamon sugar, bake in a hot oven (400°F.) about 15 minutes, until topping is glazed. Fills 8 crêpes.

Mocha Sundae Crêpes

Fill warm or cooled Blender Crêpes (page 25) with ice cream. Top with warm chocolate sauce (below) and a dab of whipped cream.

Blender Mocha Sauce

4 squares unsweetened bak-   1 teaspoon vanilla
   ing chocolate (4 oz.)   Dash salt
1 cup sugar
⅔ cup hot strong coffee

Break chocolate into blender container, add sugar and hot coffee, blend until smooth. Makes 1 cup. Keeps well in the refrigerator, can be reheated.

Cocoa Fluff Crêpes

1 cup heavy cream   ¼ cup cocoa
¼ cup confectioners' sugar   Dash salt

Make Blender Crêpes (page 25) just before serving. Put all ingredients into blender container. Turn motor on and off quickly 7 or 8 times. Stop when the cream begins to hold the line of the swirling blades. Spoon onto crêpes, roll up. Fills 12 crêpes.

4
Economy Crêpes

These Economy Crêpes (page 25) are truly economical: the batter is made with only one egg, and nonfat dry-milk solids take the place of whole milk. Yet the crêpes are as thin and delicate as the most expensive of their kind. And the fillings suggested are equally luxurious in taste, if not in price—from "caviar" made with eggplant to a rich cheesecake filling based on an instant pudding mix. Learn from other recipes in this section how to make much of little: the remains of a beef stew, stale cake crumbs, small amounts of leftover ham, turkey, or chicken. Economy Crêpes make economy meals.

Appetizer Crêpes

Eggplant Caviar Crêpes

1 medium eggplant, un-peeled	1 teaspoon salt
1 onion, grated	1 teaspoon sugar
2 tomatoes, peeled, seeded, chopped	2 tablespoons oil
	1 tablespoon lemon juice
	½ teaspoon pepper

Make Economy Crêpes (page 25), keep warm. Wash eggplant, bake in a moderate oven (350°F.) about 25 minutes or until the flesh is very soft—pulp will collapse. Cool the eggplant, strip off and discard the skin. Chop the pulp and add remaining ingredients, adjusting seasoning to taste. Spoon on crêpes, roll up. Fills about 16 crêpes.

Mixed Vegetable Crêpes

1 large onion, finely diced	1 green pepper, slivered
½ cup grated carrot	¼ cup butter or oil
½ cup shredded cabbage	Salt, cayenne

Make Economy Crêpes (page 25), browning them on one side only. Cook the vegetables in the butter or oil until the onions are translucent, about 10 minutes, stirring often. Season to taste. Use a slotted spoon to spoon vegetables onto the browned side of the crêpes, roll up. Arrange flap side down on a buttered baking dish. Sprinkle butter or oil drained from vegetables on the crêpes. Bake in a hot oven (425°F.) about 10 minutes, until the crêpes are brown and crisp. Fills about 8 crêpes.

Main Dish Crêpes

Mackerel in Blanket

1 can (about 16 ounces) mackerel	Salt, pepper, paprika
2 tablespoons butter or oil	1 tablespoon Worcestershire sauce
1 small onion, minced	1 teaspoon lemon juice

Prepare 6 Economy Crêpes (page 25), and keep warm. Drain mackerel and reserve liquid. Fillet mackerel with a fork, removing bones and skin but leaving halves intact. Heat butter or oil in skillet, brown onion, add mackerel pieces, about ½ cup liquid from can and seasonings, heat through. Spoon mackerel fillet and some of sauce onto each crêpe. Roll up and serve. Makes 3 servings.

Beef and Pepper Crêpes

1 pound ground beef	¼ cup water or beef bouillon
1 onion, chopped	½ teaspoon salt
¼ cup chopped red and green peppers	Pepper
1 tablespoon flour	

Make Economy Crêpes (page 25), keep warm. Stir beef in a skillet until it loses color, drain off excess fat. Add onion and green pepper, cook until onion is translucent. Sprinkle with flour and cook, stirring, for a moment. Add water, simmer 2 minutes. Season to taste with salt and pepper. Spoon generously onto prepared crêpes, roll. Fills 8 crêpes.

Franks and Beans Crêpes

1 can (1 pound) baked beans	1 tablespoon brown sugar
6 skinless frankfurters, cut in quarters	1 teaspoon Worcestershire sauce

Make Economy Crêpes (page 25), keep warm. Heat baked beans with frankfurters, add sugar and Worcestershire to taste, simmer until moisture evaporates. Spoon onto hot crêpes, roll up. Fills 12 crêpes.

Ham Hash Crêpes

2 cups diced cooked ham	2 stalks celery, chopped
1½ cups diced boiled potatoes	1 egg
2 tablespoons butter or margarine	1 tablespoon Worcestershire sauce
½ cup chopped onion	1 tablespoon minced parsley
½ cup chopped green pepper	Salt, pepper

Make Economy Crêpes (page 25), browning them on one side only, keep warm. Combine ham and potatoes. Melt butter or margarine, cook onion, pepper, and celery until just tender. Combine with ham-potato mixture, add egg, Worcestershire sauce, parsley, and salt and pepper to taste. Spoon generously onto browned side of crêpes, roll up. Arrange flap side down on a buttered shallow baking dish. Bake in a moderate oven (350°F.) about 15 minutes, until crêpes and hash are hot. Fills 8 crêpes.

Bean Crêpes

1 can (16 ounces) baked beans, vegetarian style	1 teaspoon garlic powder
1 tablespoon instant minced onion	2 tablespoons lemon juice
	2 tablespoons oil
½ teaspoon hot pepper sauce	¼ teaspoon ground cumin
	2 tablespoons grated Parmesan cheese

Make Economy Crêpes (page 25) in advance, if desired. Drain sauce from beans, mix beans with remaining ingredients. Adjust seasoning to taste. Spread on crêpes, roll up, arrange on a buttered shallow baking dish, sprinkle with cheese. Bake in a hot oven (400°F.) until the cheese topping browns, about 10 minutes. Fills 12 to 16 crêpes.

Sweet and Sour Meatballs in Crêpes

1 pound ground beef	2 tablespoons oil
1 tablespoon instant minced onion	¾ cup beef bouillon
	Juice of 1 lemon
1 egg yolk	¼ cup raisins
1 teaspoon salt	2 tablespoons sugar
⅛ teaspoon pepper	4 gingersnaps, crushed
Cornstarch	

Make Economy Crêpes (page 25), keep warm. Mix beef, onion, egg and salt and pepper to taste, shape into 16 walnut-sized balls. Dust with cornstarch, brown in oil in a stew pan. Add remaining ingredients except gingersnaps, cover, simmer 30 minutes. Add gingersnap crumbs, cook 5 to 7 minutes longer, until sauce is very thick—boil rapidly, if necessary, to reduce it. Adjust seasoning with more sugar and lemon, if desired. Divide meatballs onto crêpes, roll up. Spoon sauce over the rolls. Serve at once. Makes 8 crêpes.

Turkey-Stuffed Crêpes

1 can (10½ ounces) condensed cream of mushroom soup	½ cup cream or milk
	3 cups diced cooked turkey

Make Economy Crêpes (page 25). Heat soup and cream, stirring to blend. Reserve ½ cup of this sauce for topping, add remainder to turkey, heat. Spoon turkey mixture onto crêpes, roll up, arrange in buttered shallow baking dish. Top with reserved sauce, bake in a moderate oven (350°F.) about 10 to 15 minutes until crêpes and filling are piping hot. Makes about 12 crêpes.

Curried Chicken Crêpes

2 tablespoons fat	1 cup chicken bouillon
2 tablespoons chopped onion	1 cup cubed cooked chicken
2 tablespoons slivered celery	Chopped peanuts for garnish
2 tablespoons flour	
1 to 2 teaspoons curry powder	

Make Economy Crêpes (page 25) just before serving. Melt fat, add onion and celery, cook over low heat 5 minutes, until vegetables are softened. Sprinkle with flour and curry powder, cook, stirring, for a minute or two. Gradually add chicken bouillon and cook, stirring, until sauce is thick and smooth. Add chicken, heat. Spoon curry mixture onto hot crêpes, sprinkle with chopped peanuts. Fills 12 crêpes.

Crêpes Used to Line Casserole

Line the bottom and sides of a casserole with crêpes, letting the side liners hang over the edge so that they can serve partially to cover the filling. Fill casserole with any creamed mixture (usually of leftovers). Cover any bare space on top with more crêpes. Bake until hot.

Dessert Crêpes

Instant "Cheese" Dessert Crêpes

1 cup sour cream	Sour cream and brown sugar for topping
¾ cup milk	
1 package (3¾ ounces) vanilla instant pudding	

Make Economy Crêpes (page 25). Blend sour cream and milk in a mixing bowl, add vanilla pudding, beat smooth with a rotary beater. Chill until firm. Spoon onto crêpes, reheated or cool, and roll up. Serve with additional sour cream as a sauce, sprinkle top with brown sugar. Fills 16 crêpes.

Chocolate Crumb Crêpes

1 package (4 ounces) chocolate pudding mix	¼ teaspoon almond extract
	1 cup crumbled macaroons, other cookies, or dry cake
1½ cups milk	

Make Economy Crêpes (page 25). Prepare chocolate pudding according to package directions, using only 1½ cups milk. Add almond extract and cool, stirring occasionally. Stir in crumbs. Fill reheated or cool crêpes, roll up. Fills 16 crêpes.

Apple Pie Crêpes

1 jar (about 1 pound) apple pie filling	Cinnamon, lemon juice
	Confectioners' sugar

Make Economy Crêpes (page 25) in advance, as convenient. Taste apple pie filling and season to taste with cinnamon and lemon juice. Fill crêpes, roll up, dust with confectioners' sugar, arrange on a buttered shallow baking dish. Bake in a moderate oven (350°F.) about 15 minutes until crêpes are glazed and piping hot. Fills 16 crêpes.

Liqueur Cream Cheese Crêpes

½ cup whipped cream   Superfine sugar
   cheese   2 tablespoons rum
Apricot or other fruit liqueur

Make Economy Crêpes (page 25). Blend whipped cream cheese with enough apricot liqueur to make a light and fluffy mixture, divide onto crêpes, roll up. Arrange filled crêpes on a flame-proof serving dish, sprinkle them with superfine sugar, and keep warm until serving time. At the table, heat rum, ignite it, and pour it flaming over the crêpes. Makes 8 crêpes.

Crêpes with Apricot Sauce

1 jar (12 ounces) apricot   1 tablespoon butter
   preserves   2 tablespoons lemon juice
2 tablespoons water

Make Economy Crêpes (page 25), fold into quarters, keep warm. Stir apricot preserves with water over low heat, add butter, stir until hot. Add lemon juice. Spoon hot sauce over crêpes. Makes sauce for 16 crêpes.

Fruit Fillings for Crêpes

Sprinkle strawberries, raspberries, blackberries, or grapes in season with sugar and liqueur, use to fill crêpes. Or, section an apple or orange or two, and sweeten with liqueur or heated preserves, use to fill crêpes.

Dice poached pears, peaches, apricots, or plums, or use crushed pineapple; mix with macaroon crumbs. Use to fill crêpes.

5
Quick Crêpes

While any crêpes are quick to make, the combinations in this chapter are double-quick—many of them made with toppings sprinkled on the crêpes as they set in the pan, or with additions to the batter itself. Use the recipe for Quick Crêpes on page 25, based on pancake mix, or whirl the speedy Blender Crêpes batter (page 25). Or, reach into your freezer or refrigerator for previously prepared crêpes, and enjoy these treats in short order.

Appetizer Crêpes

Liver Pâté Crêpes

2 cans (about 4 ounces each) liver pâté   3 tablespoons cream cheese

Make Quick Crêpes (page 25) and keep warm. Blend liver paste and cream cheese, spread on warm crêpes. Roll up, cut in half. Fills 16 crêpes.

Tuna Caper Crêpes

1 can (7 ounces) tuna   2 tablespoons capers,
2 tablespoons mayonnaise   drained and minced
2 tablespoons sour cream

Make Quick Crêpes (page 25). Flake tuna finely, blend with remaining ingredients. Spread on hot or cold crêpes, roll up, cut in half. Makes 10 crêpes.

Shrimp Crêpes

2 scallions   Salt, pepper
¼ cup sliced water chestnuts   ¼ cup soy sauce
2 tablespoons butter   Worcestershire sauce,
½ pound peeled, deveined   Tabasco sauce
   shrimp   ¼ cup milk
1 can (10¾ ounces) con-
   densed cream of shrimp
   soup

Make Quick Crêpes (page 25). Cook scallions and water chestnuts in butter until scallions are translucent. Add shrimp, cook for 2 minutes, or until shrimp begin to turn pink. Add ¼ cup soup and seasonings to taste. Divide mixture onto crêpes, roll up, arrange flap side down on a buttered dish. Mix remaining soup with milk, soy sauce, and Worcestershire sauce and Tabasco sauce to taste. Pour over crêpes. Bake in hot oven (400°F.) about 15 minutes, until sauce is bubbling hot. Makes 10 to 12 crêpes.

Savory Sausage Crêpes

1 pound sausage links   ½ cup tomato sauce
2 tablespoons minced celery   Grated Parmesan cheese

Make Quick Crêpes (page 25). Slice sausage links, brown in a saucepan. Pour off excess fat. Add celery and tomato sauce, simmer until thickened, stirring often. Spoon onto crêpes, roll. Arrange on buttered flame-proof dish. Sprinkle lightly with grated Parmesan, place under broiler flame until cheese browns and crêpes are hot. Makes 12 crêpes.

Main Dish Crêpes

Crêpes Filled in the Pan

Sausage and Cheddar Crêpes

Make Quick Crêpes (page 25). As each crêpe begins to set, sprinkle with 1 tablespoon cooked sausage meat, 1 tablespoon grated Cheddar. Roll.

Sausage and Tomato Crêpes

Make Quick Crêpes (page 25). As each crêpe begins to set, sprinkle it with 1 tablespoon cooked sausage meat, 1 tablespoon stewed tomatoes. Roll.

Smoked Salmon Crêpes

Make Quick Crêpes (page 25). As each crêpe begins to set, sprinkle it with 1 tablespoon shredded smoked salmon. Roll. Serve with tartar sauce or whipped cream cheese.

Quick Lobster Crêpes

8 ounces (about 1 cup) fresh, canned, or frozen lobster meat, cooked   1 cup sliced fresh mushrooms (or canned, drained)
1 tablespoon chopped green onions   ¼ cup butter
   Salt, pepper

Make Quick Crêpes (page 25), keep warm. Pick over lobster meat, discarding any membranes. Cook onions and mushrooms in butter until onion is translucent. Add lobster, heat. Adjust seasoning with salt and pepper. Spoon onto crêpes, roll. Fills 8 to 12 crêpes.

Variation: Add to the butter ½ to 1 teaspoon curry powder, to taste.

Bacon or Ham Crêpes

½ to 1 cup crisp bacon crumbles   or ½ to 1 cup slivered cooked ham

Add bacon or ham to Quick Crêpes batter (page 25), cook crêpes as directed. Serve, sprinkled with coarsely ground black pepper.

Variation on this theme: Substitute diced cooked chicken or turkey for half the ham or bacon in this recipe.

Another variation: Cook ½ pound sausage meat until browned, stirring constantly with a fork to break up the meat. Drain off fat. Add sausage to prepared Quick Crêpe batter (page 25), make crêpes as directed.

Onion Crêpes

1 cup chopped onion
2 tablespoons butter

Sour cream

Make batter for Quick Crêpes (page 25). Cook onion in butter until translucent. Add to batter. Cook crêpes as directed, roll up, serve with a topping of sour cream. Makes 12 crêpes.

Dessert Crêpes

Apricot Crêpes

1 jar (12 ounces) apricot preserves
2 tablespoons lemon juice

2 tablespoons water
1 tablespoon butter
¼ cup slivered almonds

Make Quick Crêpes (page 25), turning once to brown both sides. Fold crêpes into quarters. In skillet, heat preserves with lemon juice, water, and butter. Add crêpes, turn in sauce to heat through. Garnish with almonds. Makes 16 to 20 crêpes.

Cherry Pie Crêpes

1 can (1 pound) cherry pie filling
½ teaspoon almond extract

Dash powdered cloves
Heavy cream for topping (optional)

Make Quick Crêpes (page 25). Warm cherry pie filling, season with almond extract and cloves to taste. Fill hot crêpes, serve plain or topped with whipped cream. Fills 16 crêpes.

Variations: Use apple pie filling and heat with ¼ cup raisins; or add chopped nuts and a dash of nutmeg. Use blueberry pie filling, brightened with grated orange or lemon rind.

Banana Crêpes Filled in the Pan

Make Quick Crêpes (page 25). As each crêpe begins to set, add 1 tablespoon mashed banana, a few drops lemon juice. Roll, sprinkle with confectioners' sugar and chopped nuts.

Cream Cheese Crêpes Filled in the Pan

Soften 1 package (8 ounces) cream cheese at room temperature, whip with 1 tablespoon or more milk to make a fluffy mixture. When crêpe begins to set, add spoonful of cheese, roll. Serve garnished with a little marmalade. Makes enough for 16 crêpes.

6
French Fines Herbes Crêpes

Fines Herbes Crêpes (page 25), made with herb-flavored batter, set off savory fillings to make appetizers and main dishes of subtle sophistication. Veal and Ham Crêpes worthy of the Cordon Bleu, Mushrooms in Cream Sauce, Turbans of Sole Mousseline and Crêpes Diane—with Fines Herbes Crêpes, you can wrap up a meal worthy of a great chef!

Appetizer Crêpes

Tower of Crêpes

¾ cup mayonnaise
¾ cup sour cream
Fillings:
¼ pound thinly sliced ham
¼ pound thinly sliced
  cooked chicken
3 hard cooked eggs, sliced
  thin
¼ pound thinly sliced Swiss
  cheese (or other)

1 small jar (1¾ ounces) red
  caviar, drained
1 small container favorite
  "sandwich spread"
½ cup chopped mushrooms,
  cooked with 2 tablespoons
  butter
2 ounces thinly sliced
  smoked salmon

Make large Fines Herbes Crêpes (page 25), or rich crêpes, or other crêpes suitable for savory snacking, to your taste. Cool. Arrange one crêpe on serving platter, spread thinly with mayonnaise combined with sour cream and a layer of filling. Cover with a second crêpe, and repeat until all the crêpes are used, with a different, but compatible filling on each. "Ice" top and sides of the tower with more mayonnaise mixture and chill well. Garnish the platter with pimiento-stuffed olives, radishes, and sprigs of watercress or parsley. Serve in slender, pie-shaped wedges as hors d'oeuvre. Serves 10 to 12.

Avocado and Chicken Liver Pâté Crêpes

1 small onion, minced
3 tablespoons butter
¾ pound chicken livers
½ pound butter
Salt, pepper, and nutmeg to
  taste

1 avocado, peeled and
  quartered
Cornichons (French midget
  pickled gherkins)
Pickled cocktail onions

Make Fines Herbes Crêpes (page 25) and refrigerate, covered. Cook onion in butter until translucent. Add livers and cook until they lose their red color, about 2 minutes. Place livers and sauce in pan in a blender container and puree at high speed for one minute. Add butter, spices, and avocado bit by bit, to make a smooth paste, chill overnight. Spread crêpes with pâté and roll up. Serve at room temperature with cornichons and pickled onions. Makes about 16 crêpes.

Cheese Crêpes Batons

12 thin slices prosciutto or
  Italian-style ham
8 ounces garlic- or herb-
  flavored Boursin-type
  cheese

2 tablespoons heavy cream
½ teaspoon freshly ground
  black pepper

Makes Fines Herbes Crêpes (page 25) and place one slice of prosciutto on each. Mix cheese with heavy cream and freshly ground black pepper. Spread mixture on prosciutto and roll crêpe up jelly-roll fashion. Arrange on a serving platter, cover and chill at least 2 hours before serving. Makes 12 crêpes.

Cream Cheese and Green Pea Crêpes

8 ounces peas, fresh or
  frozen
4 tablespoons butter, softened
8 ounces softened cream
  cheese
1 tablespoon heavy cream

¼ teaspoon chopped,
  fresh mint
Salt and freshly ground
  black pepper to taste
Pinch each of nutmeg, sugar
1 clove garlic, finely minced

Make Fines Herbes Crêpes (page 25). Cook peas in enough boiling, salted water to cover until tender. Drain, refresh in cold water, and drain again. In a blender or food mill, puree peas, butter, cream cheese, heavy cream, mint, salt, pepper, nutmeg, sugar, and garlic. Spread evenly on crêpes and roll up. Arrange on a serving platter, cover, and chill at least 2 hours before serving. Makes about 16 crêpes.

Main Dish Crêpes

Veal and Ham Filled Crêpes

½ pound veal, chopped
2 tablespoons butter
¼ pound prosciutto ham,
  chopped
3 eggs

3 tablespoons grated
  Romano cheese
Salt, pepper, paprika
1 jar (2 cups) prepared
  spaghetti sauce

Make Fines Herbes Crêpes (page 25) in advance, if convenient. Cook veal in butter, stirring constantly, 5 minutes. Add ham, cook 5 minutes longer. Beat eggs with cheese, add veal and ham. Season to taste with salt, pepper, and paprika. Divide mixture onto crêpes, fold up. Pour spaghetti sauce into a shallow baking dish, arrange rolls on sauce, folded side down, sprinkle with more grated cheese, if desired. Bake in a hot oven (400°F.) about 15 minutes, until the topping melts and the sauce is bubbling hot. Makes about 6 servings.

Crêpe Roulade of Ham and Kumquats

½ cup cooked ham, diced
½ cup kumquats
2 teaspoons hot mustard
2 tablespoons mayonnaise
1 teaspoon curry powder
2 egg yolks
½ cup pecans or almonds,
  chopped

¼ cup pickled watermelon
  rind, cut in ½-inch cubes
½ teaspoon salt
1 teaspoon Dijon-style
  mustard
¼ cup maple syrup
1 teaspoon cider vinegar

Make Fines Herbes Crêpes (page 25). Whirl ham, kumquats, hot mustard, mayonnaise, curry powder, egg yolks in a blender until smooth. Combine with pecans, watermelon rind, and salt. Divide the mixture onto the crêpes. Roll up and place side by side in a shallow baking dish. Brush tops with Dijon-style mustard. Mix maple syrup and vinegar and pour over crêpes. Bake in a hot oven (425°F.) for 15 minutes, until crêpes are puffed and lightly browned. Makes about 8 crêpes.

Chicken and Duxelles Crêpes

½ pound mushrooms, finely minced	2 cups cooked chicken, cut in ¾-inch cubes
1 small onion, finely minced	6 tablespoons heavy cream
6 tablespoons butter	1 egg yolk
Salt and pepper to taste	½ cup heavy cream
Pinch each of nutmeg and thyme	2 tablespoons chopped parsley

Make Fines Herbes Crêpes (page 25). Cook mushrooms and onions in butter, stirring occasionally, until vegetables are very tender and all excess moisture has evaporated. Remove from heat and combine with the salt, pepper, nutmeg, thyme, cooked chicken, 6 tablespoons heavy cream, and egg yolk. Spoon onto crêpes, roll up and arrange, side by side, in a shallow baking dish. Top with ½ cup heavy cream, cover with wax paper, and bake in a 400°F. oven for 15 minutes, until hot. Sprinkle with parsley and serve. Makes about 8 crêpes.

Turbans of Sole Mousseline

6 fillets of sole (8 ounces each)	⅛ teaspoon thyme
3 tablespoons butter	1 cup white sauce (preferably a fish velouté)
2 small carrots, finely diced	2 egg yolks
1 small onion, finely diced	½ cup heavy cream, whipped
2 ribs celery, finely diced	
Salt, pepper	

Make 6 large Fines Herbes Crêpes (page 25). Place one fish fillet on each crêpe. Heat butter in a heavy-bottomed saucepan, add carrots, onion, and celery, and cook, stirring occasionally, until vegetables are just tender. Add salt, pepper, and thyme. Cool slightly and spread on fish fillets. Fold sides of crêpe over the filling, and arrange side by side in a shallow baking dish, folded side down. Bring white sauce to a simmer, remove from heat, and beat in egg yolks. Quickly fold in whipped cream. Pour sauce over

crêpes, bake in hot oven (425°F.) for 10 minutes, until hot and golden brown. Serves 6.

Lobster Thermidor Crêpes

4 tablespoons butter	Pinch dry mustard
2 tablespoons shallots (or green onions) finely minced	1 cup Béchamel Sauce (below)
1 cup mushrooms, coarsely minced	1 pound cooked lobster meat, cut into ½-inch pieces
2 large ripe tomatoes, peeled, seeded, and chopped	2 tablespoons brandy
¼ cup dry sherry or Madeira	1 ripe avocado, peeled and cut into ½-inch pieces
1 teaspoon salt	½ cup heavy cream, whipped
¼ teaspoon each pepper, paprika	

Make Fines Herbes Crêpes (page 25). Melt butter in a heavy-bottomed saucepan. Add shallots, mushrooms, and tomatoes and cook 4 minutes, stirring occasionally. Add sherry, salt, pepper, paprika, mustard, ½ cup Béchamel Sauce, and the lobster meat. Blend well, simmer 5 minutes longer. Remove from heat, stir in brandy, and gently fold in the avocado. Cool mixture and divide onto crêpes. Roll up and arrange side by side in a shallow baking dish. Combine remaining Béchamel Sauce with whipped cream, pour over crêpes. Bake in hot oven (425°F.) for 15 minutes, until topping is golden brown. Fills about 12 crêpes.

Béchamel Sauce

2 tablespoons butter	Pinch nutmeg
1 small onion, minced	¼ teaspoon salt
3 tablespoons flour	Pinch white pepper
2 cups scalded milk	

Melt butter in a heavy-bottomed saucepan. Cook onions until translucent. Add flour and cook, stirring constantly, until the mixture foams. Quickly stir in scalded milk, nutmeg, salt, and pepper. Cook, stirring, until sauce is thickened. Strain through a fine sieve and dot with butter to prevent a skin from forming. Makes about 2 cups.

Crêpes Diane

6 tablespoons butter	2 teaspoons Dijon-style mustard
4 slices sirloin cut ¼-inch thick and pounded into paper-thin 5-inch circles	2 tablespoons Worcestershire sauce
Salt and freshly ground black pepper to taste	¼ cup prepared brown sauce
2 tablespoons butter	Dry sherry to taste
¾ cup finely minced shallots or green onions	Juice of ¼ lemon
	1 tablespoon butter

Make 4 large Fines Herbes Crêpes (page 25). Heat 2 tablespoons butter until bubbling in a heavy-bottomed skillet and quickly sear steaks on both sides, adding more butter as necessary. As each steak is seared, remove it from the pan and sprinkle with salt and pepper. Place one steak on each crêpe and roll up. Arrange filled crêpes side by side in a shallow, oven-proof serving dish. Cover and set in a slow oven (225°F.) to keep warm. Meanwhile, drain butter from pan, add 2 tablespoons butter and the shallots. Cook, stirring constantly, 3 minutes. Blend in mustard, Worcestershire sauce, and brown sauce, and cook until thickened. Stir in sherry, lemon juice, and butter, adjust seasonings, and pour over warm crêpes. Makes 4 servings.

Crêpe Sandwiches Monte Cristo

4 tablespoons Dijon-style mustard	¼ pound Swiss cheese, thinly sliced
¾ pound cooked chicken breast, thinly sliced	3 eggs, beaten
¼ pound cooked, smoked ham, thinly sliced	6 tablespoons butter

Make Fines Herbes Crêpes (page 25), brown on one side only. Spread 1 teaspoon mustard on the browned side of each crêpe and top with a slice of chicken, a slice of ham, and a slice of cheese. Roll crêpes up jelly-roll fashion, dip in beaten eggs, and sauté in hot butter until golden brown. Fills about 12 crêpes.

Mushroom Crêpes

1 small onion, finely minced	Pinch nutmeg
1 pound mushrooms, finely minced	2 tablespoons heavy cream
3 tablespoons butter	2 eggs, lightly beaten
½ teaspoon salt	½ cup fine dry bread crumbs
¼ teaspoon freshly ground black pepper	¼ cup butter
	2 tablespoons parsley

Make Fines Herbes Crêpes (page 25), browning one side only. Sauté onions and mushrooms in butter until most of the liquid is evaporated. Season with salt, pepper, and nutmeg. Add heavy cream, cool. Divide mixture onto the browned side of the crêpes. Fold the sides over the filling and roll up to form an envelope. Dip into beaten eggs and roll in crumbs. Gently sauté breaded crêpes in butter until browned on all sides. Remove to serving platter and sprinkle with parsley. Fills about 16 crêpes.

7

French Almond Crêpes

Choose one or more of these elegant crêpes for a party or special dinner or dessert treat. Almond Crêpes (page 25) with distinctive flavor and texture demand fillings with discriminating gourmet appeal. These are crêpes to linger over, in the making and the tasting! Serve with your best wines, at your finest table setting.

Appetizer Crêpes

Chicken Mousse Crêpes

3 cups cooked chicken, cut up
1 envelope unflavored gelatin
1½ cups cold chicken stock
2 eggs, separated
½ cup heavy cream
3 tablespoons Madeira or brandy

Make two batches of French Almond Crêpes (page 25). Grind chicken several times through the finest blade of a meat grinder. Soften gelatin in ½ cup cold chicken stock. Heat the remaining stock, stir in the gelatin mixture, stir over heat until clear. Beat egg yolks, combine with gelatin mixture, and cook, stirring constantly, until sauce is thickened somewhat. Do not boil. Set aside to cool. Beat egg whites stiff, then whip heavy cream. Mix together ground chicken, the thickened chicken stock, and whipped cream. Stir in Madeira and fold in the egg whites. Spoon filling on crêpes and roll up. Arrange seam side down in serving dish, cover, chill at least 3 hours. Makes about 32 crêpes.

Sole Mousse Crêpes

1 pound fillets of sole
¾ teaspoon salt
⅛ teaspoon white pepper
Pinch nutmeg
2 egg whites
2 cups heavy cream
Soft butter

Make French Almond Crêpes (page 25), browning on one side only. Whirl fish in a blender with salt, pepper, and nutmeg to make a very fine puree. Gradually add the egg whites. Cover and chill 2 to 3 hours. Add cream, a little at a time, stirring with a wooden spoon. Butter the unbrowned side of crêpes, spoon on 3 tablespoons of mousse mixture, roll up. Place crêpes in a buttered baking dish. Bake in a moderate oven (350°F.) for 25 minutes, or until mousse is puffed and golden brown. Makes 24 crêpes.

Crêpes aux Huitres aux Amandes (Oyster Crêpes with Almonds)

¼ cup sweet butter
¼ cup finely ground blanched almonds
1 clove garlic, minced
1½ teaspoons brandy
Pinch cayenne
1 dozen oysters, freshly shucked
2 tablespoons chopped parsley

Make French Almond Crêpes (page 25). Cream butter, blend with almonds, garlic, brandy, and cayenne. Place one oyster on each crêpe, cover with 1 tablespoon almond-butter mixture, and sprinkle with parsley. Roll up crêpes and place in a buttered baking dish. Bake 10 minutes in a hot oven (400°F.). Makes 12 crêpes.

Quick Liver Pâté Crêpes

½ pound smoked liverwurst
½ cup softened butter
2 tablespoons minced shallots
1 tablespoon parsley
1 tablespoon brandy

Make French Almond Crêpes (page 25). Mix all ingredients thoroughly to make a smooth pâté. Spread liver pâté on crêpes and roll up. Cover and refrigerate overnight. Serve with cornichons (French pickles) and pickled onions. Makes 16 crêpes.

Main Dish Crêpes

Creamed Chicken and Almond Crêpes

4 tablespoons butter
4 tablespoons flour
2 cups chicken stock
1 cup light cream
Salt, pepper, and nutmeg to taste
1 cup mushroom caps, quartered
2 cups cubed raw chicken
½ cup toasted almonds

Make French Almond Crêpes (page 25). Melt butter, add flour, and cook, stirring constantly, until golden brown. Stir in chicken stock, cream, and seasonings. Cook, stirring occasionally, until thickened. Reserve 1½ cups sauce. To remaining sauce, add mushrooms, chicken, and almonds. Simmer 25 minutes, until chicken is just cooked. Cool to room temperature. Spoon onto crêpes and roll up. Place crêpes side by side in a buttered casserole and top with reserved sauce. Bake in a hot oven (425°F.) 15 minutes, or until lightly browned and bubbling hot. Makes 16 crêpes.

French Peas Crêpes

1 pound fresh green peas
4 strips bacon, diced
2 tablespoons butter
¼ head lettuce, shredded
Juice of one lemon
Salt and pepper to taste
Butter
Parmesan cheese

Make French Almond Crêpes (page 25). Cook peas in boiling salted water until just tender. Drain. Or, use 1 package frozen small peas, cooked as directed. Sauté bacon in butter until golden brown. Stir in lettuce, drained peas, lemon juice, and seasonings. Cook, stirring occasionally, until lettuce is wilted. Spoon mixture onto crêpes and roll up. Arrange in baking dish, dot with butter, and sprinkle with Parmesan cheese. Bake in a hot oven (425°F.) until topping is golden brown. Makes 4 to 6 servings.

Trout Crêpes

4 small fresh trout	½ cup heavy cream
Flour for dredging	Cayenne
4 tablespoons butter	2 tablespoons chopped
2 tablespoons oil	parsley
½ cup blanched, slivered	
almonds	

Make 4 large French Almond Crêpes (page 25). Clean, wash, and dry 4 fresh trout. Dip lightly in flour and quickly sauté in hot butter and oil. Remove browned trout, slip out center bone, wrap each fish loosely in a crêpe. Sauté almonds in remaining butter until toasted. Stir in heavy cream and cayenne to taste, cook rapidly to reduce sauce by one-fourth. Pour over crêpes and sprinkle with parsley. Makes 4 servings.

Crêpes Benedict
(Crêpes, Poached Eggs, and Hollandaise Sauce)

4 cups water	1 tablespoon butter
½ cup vinegar	1 cup Hollandaise sauce
6 eggs	(below)
6 slices Canadian bacon	

Make French Almond Crêpes (page 25). Combine water and vinegar. Bring to a rolling boil, turn down heat. Slip eggs, one at a time, from a saucer into the simmering water, poach until white is opaque but yolks still soft. Sauté bacon until lightly browned. Arrange a slice of bacon on each crêpe, top with a poached egg. Roll crêpes up carefully and place in a buttered oven-proof casserole dish. Top crêpes with Hollandaise sauce and quickly glaze under the broiler. Makes 6 crêpes.

Hollandaise Sauce

3 egg yolks	Pinch white pepper or dash
2 teaspoons hot water	of Tabasco sauce
1 teaspoon white wine	¾ cup melted butter
vinegar	Juice of ½ lemon
½ teaspoon salt	

Beat egg yolks, water, vinegar, salt, and pepper in a glass or ceramic bowl, set over a pan of slowly simmering water, and cook, beating constantly with whisk, until mixture is the consistency of custard. Remove the bowl and slowly beat in melted butter, drop by drop at first, and then in a thin stream. Add lemon juice, adjust seasonings if necessary. Serve warm or keep at room temperature until ready to serve. Makes 1½ cups.

Crêpes Cordon Bleu

1 pound veal cutlets (6	½ pound Gruyère cheese,
pieces)	sliced
Flour for dredging	2 eggs, beaten
½ cup oil	1 cup finely ground bread
¼ pound prosciutto, thinly	crumbs
sliced	

Make French Almond Crêpes (page 25). Pound cutlets between sheets of wax paper to a uniform thickness of ¼ inch. Dredge in flour. Heat oil almost to smoking and quickly brown veal on both sides. Place one cutlet on each crêpe, top with a slice of prosciutto and a slice of Gruyère, fold crêpe over to enclose filling. Dust the crêpes with flour, dip in beaten egg, and coat with bread crumbs. Increase heat under pan. In the pan in which the veal was cooked, brown crêpes on both sides. Serve as is, or top with Hollandaise Sauce (this page). Makes 6 crêpes.

Dessert Crêpes

Crêpes Pithiviers

⅓ cup blanched almonds	¼ cup rum
6 tablespoons superfine	2 tablespoons flour
sugar	2 tablespoons butter
3 tablespoons softened butter	2 tablespoons sugar
2 eggs	

Make French Almond Crêpes (page 25). Combine almonds, sugar, and butter in a blender and whirl to a smooth paste. Remove to a small bowl and stir in eggs, one at a time. Add rum and flour. Spoon almond mixture on crêpes, roll up loosely and arrange, side by side, in buttered baking dish. Dot with butter and sprinkle with sugar. Bake, covered, in a preheated oven (350°F.) 20 to 25 minutes. Makes 8 crêpes.

Crêpes Malakoff
(Almond Butter Cream)

¼ pound almonds	1 ounce kirsch
¼ pound confectioners'	1 cup whipped cream, beaten
sugar	stiff
1 tsp. vanilla	Confectioners' sugar
¼ pound softened butter	

Make French Almond Crêpes (page 25), adding 2 tablespoons sugar to crêpe batter, if desired. Meanwhile whirl almonds in a blender to make a fine powder. Transfer nuts to a mixing bowl and stir in sugar and vanilla. Add the softened butter and kirsch and blend into a smooth paste. Gently fold in whipped cream. Spoon onto crêpes and roll up. Arrange side by side on a serving dish and sprinkle with confectioners' sugar. Cover and refrigerate until serving time. Makes 16 crêpes.

Crêpes Grandgousier
(Hot Applesauce and Rum)

2½ cups thick applesauce	2 tablespoons butter
1 teaspoon finely grated	¼ cup rum
lemon zest	¼ cup superfine sugar
Nutmeg to taste	

If desired, add 2 tablespoons rum to the batter for French Almond Crêpes (page 25). To applesauce, add lemon zest, nutmeg, butter, and rum. Cook over moderate heat, stirring occasionally, until the mixture is as thick as apple butter. Spoon filling onto crêpes, roll up, and arrange on an oven-proof platter. Sprinkle crêpes with sugar and set in a hot oven (400°F.) for a few minutes, until sugar is caramelized. Makes 16 crêpes.

Macaroon Crêpes

⅔ cup blanched almonds	Vanilla
2 egg whites, lightly beaten	2 tablespoons butter
⅔ cup sugar	

Make French Almond Crêpes (page 25). In a blender, whirl almonds until they are as fine as sugar. Remove to a mixing bowl, and beat in egg whites and sugar alternately, beginning and ending with egg white. Add vanilla to taste. Spoon filling onto crêpes and roll loosely. Arrange crêpes side by side in a buttered, oven-proof serving dish. Bake, covered, in a moderate (350°F.) oven for 20 minutes. Makes about 16 crêpes.

Frangipane Crêpes
(Almond Pastry Cream)

½ cup sugar	3 cups scalded milk
¾ cup flour	3 tablespoons butter
Pinch salt	½ cup pulverized almonds
2 whole eggs	1 teaspoon almond extract
2 egg yolks	¼ cup confectioners' sugar

Make French Almond Crêpes (page 25). Combine sugar, flour, and salt in a heavy-bottomed saucepan. Add eggs and mix thoroughly with a wooden spoon. Add the scalded milk in a thin stream, mixing while you pour. Cook over low-moderate heat, stirring constantly, until custard is thickened or about 4 or 5 minutes. Strain through a sieve or foodmill and stir in the butter, almonds, and almond extract. Spoon onto each crêpe and roll up. Serve warm sprinkled with confectioners' sugar. Makes about 16 crêpes.

Crêpes Glacé aux Marrons

1 pint vanilla ice cream	2 cups compote de marrons (canned chestnuts in a vanilla syrup)

Make French Almond Crêpes (page 25). If desired, add 2 tablespoons sugar to the crêpe batter. Allow crêpes to cool, spoon 4 tablespoons ice cream onto each crêpe and roll up. Arrange crêpes on aluminum foil, seal tightly and set in freezer compartment until ready to serve. Heat up the chestnut sauce (compote de marrons) and spoon ¼ cup over each crêpe. Makes 8 crêpes.

8
French Chocolate Crêpes

The chocolate is in the crêpes in these desserts made with Chocolate Crêpes batter (page 25). These new, delicate, and flavorful crêpes are filled with Chocolate Butter Cream, Crème Pâtissière, Crème Chantilly, sauced with flaming chocolate . . . temptations to turn any dessert lover's head.

Dessert Crêpes

Crème Chantilly Crêpes

1 cup heavy cream   1 teaspoon vanilla
¼ cup confectioners' sugar

Make French Chocolate Crêpes (page 25). Whip cream with sugar until stiff. Fold in vanilla. Fill warm or cold crêpes and roll. Makes 16 crêpes.

Chocolate Butter Cream Crêpes

2 tablespoons soft butter	Pinch salt
1 cup sifted confectioners' sugar	1 egg yolk
1 teaspoon milk	1 envelope liquid unsweetened chocolate (or 1-ounce square, melted)
1 teaspoon vanilla	

Make French Chocolate Crêpes (page 25). Cream butter with sugar. Beat in milk, vanilla, and salt. Add egg yolk, chocolate, and more sugar, if necessary, to make a fluffy mixture that will hold its shape. Spread on warm or cooled crêpes, roll up. Makes 8 crêpes.

Crêpes au Crème Pâtissière
(Pastry Cream Crêpes)

1½ cups milk	2 egg yolks
½ cup sugar	½ teaspoon vanilla
¼ cup flour	Confectioners' sugar or
2 eggs	Slivered almonds for topping

Make French Chocolate Crêpes (page 25), keep warm or let cool. Scald milk. Mix sugar and flour in the top of a double boiler off the heat. Add eggs and egg yolks, beat well. Stir in milk and cook over hot water, stirring constantly, until mixture reaches the boiling point. Cool, stirring often. Add vanilla. Spoon mixture onto crêpes, roll. Dust with powdered sugar or sprinkle with slivered almonds. Makes 16 crêpes.

Flaming Chocolate Sauce for Crêpes

1 cup (6 ounces) semisweet chocolate pieces	½ cup sour cream
	¼ cup Bourbon

Make French Chocolate Crêpes (page 25), fold into quarters. Melt chocolate pieces in a small pan over hot water. Stir in sour cream. Heat Bourbon in ladle and ignite it. Pour blazing into hot sauce. Pour flaming sauce over crêpes. Makes about 12 crêpes.

Crêpes Hélène
(Pear Crêpes)

1 can (1 pound) pears	1 tablespoon light corn syrup
1 cup semisweet chocolate pieces (6 ounces)	¼ cup cream
1 tablespoon butter	3 tablespoons brandy

Make French Chocolate Crêpes (page 25), fold into quarters. Insert a pear wedge into the top fold. Melt chocolate pieces with butter in a small pan over hot water. Gradually stir in remaining ingredients, pour over filled crêpes. Makes 16 crêpes.

Crêpes Glacés au Chocolat
(Ice Cream Crêpes with Chocolate Sauce)

Fill crêpes with ice cream, roll up, cover with the chocolate sauce for Crêpes Hélène.

Apricot Whip Crêpes

1¾ cups stewed apricots, with syrup	1 cup heavy cream
2 egg whites, whipped stiff	¼ cup confectioners' sugar
	½ teaspoon almond extract

Make double batch of French Chocolate Crêpes (page 25). Force apricots through a sieve or whirl in blender. Fold in whipped egg whites. Whip cream with sugar and almond extract, fold in. Fill hot or cold crêpes. Roll. Makes filling for 24 crêpes.

Meringue-Filled Crêpes Flambé

4 egg whites	½ cup chopped toasted almonds
¾ cup sugar	
2 tablespoons orange liqueur	¼ cup brandy

Make French Chocolate Crêpes (page 25). Beat egg whites until soft peaks form. Gradually beat in sugar until mixture stands in stiff peaks. Fold in orange liqueur. Spread crêpes with meringue, sprinkle with toasted almonds, roll. Arrange crêpes in top pan of chafing dish or flameproof serving dish. Warm brandy, ignite, pour blazing over the crêpes. Makes 16 crêpes.

Lemon Mousse Crêpes

2 lemons	⅔ cup sugar
3 eggs, separated	1½ tablespoon water

Make French Chocolate Crêpes (page 25). Grate the zest of 1 lemon, squeeze the juice from both. In the top of a double boiler, mix juice and zest with egg yolks. Add sugar and water. Put the pan over hot water and cook, stirring, until the sauce is thickened and smooth, on the point of boiling. Cool. Beat the egg whites stiff, fold in. Chill until serving time. Spoon mousse mixture onto crêpes, roll. Or, stack crêpes with layers of mousse as filling between them to make a layered gatêau. Fills 12 to 16 crêpes or layers.

Crème Brûlée Crêpes

6 tablespoons sugar	Dash salt
3 tablespoons cornstarch	2 teaspoons vanilla
3 egg yolks	¾ cup light brown sugar,
3 cups milk	sifted

Make French Chocolate Crêpes (page 25), fold into quarters. Fit the crêpes into individual custard cups, spread to make a pocket to hold the filling. Mix sugar, cornstarch, and egg yolks in a saucepan. Gradually add milk and cook, stirring constantly, until the custard thickens and begins to bubble. Add salt and vanilla. Cool, stirring frequently. Spoon custard into crêpe-lined custard cups, sprinkle with brown sugar. Place under the broiler flame until sugar melts and caramelizes. Makes 12 crêpe cups.

Pineapple Cream Crêpes

½ teaspoon gelatin	½ cup crushed pineapple,
1 tablespoon cold water	well-drained
⅓ cup heavy cream	
3 tablespoons confectioners' sugar	

Prepare French Chocolate Crêpes (page 25). Soften gelatin in cold water, place over boiling water and stir until dissolved. Cool. Combine with cream and confectioners' sugar. Beat until stiff. Fold in pineapple. Fill hot or cold crêpes. Roll. Makes about 12 crêpes.

Chocolate Mousse Crêpes

2 egg whites	6 oz. semisweet chocolate,
½ cup sugar	melted
⅛ teaspoon cream of tartar	1 cup heavy cream, whipped
¼ cup water	

Prepare French Chocolate Crêpes (page 25). Beat egg whites stiff. Stir sugar, cream of tartar and water until dissolved, then boil until it reaches the soft ball stage (232°F. on a candy thermometer). Add cooked sugar mixture in a thin stream to egg whites, blending at slow speed until cooled. Fold in cooled, melted chocolate, then whipped cream. Fill hot or cold crêpes. Roll. Makes 16 crêpes.

Banana and Cream Crêpes

1 banana	Chopped almonds or walnuts
½ cup whipped cream, sweetened and flavored with almond extract	¼ cup chocolate syrup

Prepare French Chocolate Crêpes (page 25). Slice banana, combine lightly with whipped cream. Spoon onto 2 cold or warm crêpes, sprinkle with nuts. Roll. Top with chocolate syrup. Fills two crêpes.

9
Chinese Crêpes

Chinese Crêpes (page 26) are possibly the most exotic in the world. The Chinese Eggroll, or Spring Roll, as this more delicate version is properly called, is possibly the one Chinese dish familiar to most Americans. The batter for the "wrappers," as the Chinese call them, includes cornstarch, and the crêpes it makes are delicate and tender in texture, pale in color. Deep frying gives the filled crêpes their characteristic crunchiness. The fillings are subtly flavored and demonstrate the contrasts of sharp and sweet, soft and crisp, that are typical of Chinese cooking. Serve these crêpes as one course of a Chinese meal or as a cocktail-party or teatime snack.

Appetizer Crêpes

Sweet and Pungent Pork Crêpes

1 pound tender pork, cut into ¾-inch cubes	2 teaspoons soy sauce
1 egg white, lightly beaten	1 can (about 1 pound) pineapple chunks
Cornstarch, salt	1 cup water
¼ cup vinegar	2 tablespoons cornstarch
¼ cup sherry	1 green pepper, sliced
¼ cup brown sugar	1 carrot, sliced paper thin
1 tablespoon molasses	

Cook Chinese Crêpes (page 26), on both sides, keep warm. Use pork loin fillet for this dish. Cut the meat into uniform cubes. Coat with egg white, dredge with cornstarch and salt. Let stand while you prepare the sauce. Combine vinegar, sherry, sugar, molasses, soy sauce, and the syrup drained from the canned pineapple. Add ¾ cup water, bring to a boil. Stir cornstarch with remaining water, add to pan. Cook, stirring constantly, until the sauce is clear and thickened. Add ½ can pineapple, green pepper, and carrot, simmer 5 minutes. Fry the cornstarch-coated pork cubes in deep hot fat (375°F.) until golden. Drain on paper towels. Combine with prepared sauce. Spoon pork, fruit, and vegetables onto crêpes, using a slotted spoon. Roll. Cover with sauce, garnish with remaining pineapple, serve hot. Makes 16 crêpes.

Shrimps Szechuan Crêpes

HOT SAUCE	FILLING
2 teaspoons hot brown bean sauce (or substitute meat glaze)	¼ cup oil
	4 large garlic cloves, crushed
2 tablespoons ketchup	2 tablespoons grated onion
1 teaspoon sherry	½ teaspoon dried hot peppers, crushed
2 tablespoons water	1 pound peeled, deveined shrimp
½ teaspoon sugar	Cornstarch, water for paste

Make Chinese Crêpes (page 26), cook until barely set. Prepare sauce by blending ingredients in a small bowl. For the filling, heat oil, stir garlic and onion for a minute over high heat. Add red pepper and shrimp, cook for 1 minute. Add Hot Sauce, stir over high heat until shrimp are thoroughly coated with sauce. Spoon onto crêpes, fold bottom of crêpe over filling, fold up sides, roll up. Seal flap with a little cornstarch mixed with water. Fry in deep hot fat (375°F.) until crisp and brown. Makes 16 crêpes.

Spring Rolls with Pork and Sprouts

1 pound pork, finely shredded	2 tablespoons soy sauce
3 tablespoons oil or lard	1 teaspoon sugar
3 scallions, shredded	Salt
2 cups bean sprouts, blanched	Cornstarch, water for paste

Make Chinese Crêpes (page 26). Cook pork in oil, stirring constantly, until shreds lose their red color. Add scallions and bean sprouts, stir-fry 2 minutes. Add soy sauce, sugar, and salt to taste. Spoon mixture onto lower half of browned side of Chinese crêpes. Fold bottom of crêpe over filling, fold in sides, roll up. Mix cornstarch with a little water and use this paste to seal the flap. Fry in deep hot fat (375°F.) until crisp and golden brown. Makes about 16 crêpes.

Variations: chopped shrimp may be substituted for part or all of the pork. Or, add dried mushrooms, soaked in water and shredded.

Spring Rolls with Chicken

Half a chicken breast, shredded	½ onion, slivered finely
2 teaspoons cornstarch	½ pound spinach leaves, washed and cut
1 teaspoon sugar	1 can (1 pound) bean sprouts, drained
1 teaspoon soy sauce	Cornstarch, water for paste
¼ cup oil	

Make Chinese Crêpes (page 26), browning lightly on one side only. Toss shredded chicken with cornstarch, sugar, and soy sauce. Let stand. Heat oil, add onion and spinach, stir over high heat until wilted, about 3 minutes. Add bean sprouts, stir. Remove vegetables from pan with slotted spoon, draining well. Add chicken to pan, stir over high heat until shreds are opaque. Return vegetables to pan, stir to blend. Drain off excess liquid through a colander. Cool filling, place on browned side of Chinese Crêpes. Fold up, seal with paste of cornstarch and water, fry in deep hot fat (375°F.) until crisp and golden brown. Makes about 16 crêpes.

Spring Rolls with Crab

1 pound crab meat	2 tablespoons soy sauce
2 tablespoons oil	2 tablespoons sherry
½ onion, slivered	Salt
½ teaspoon grated fresh ginger root	Cornstarch, water for paste

Make Chinese Crêpes (page 26), cook until barely set. Shred crab, discard any shells or tendons. Heat oil, add crab, onion, and ginger, stir-fry for a minute over medium heat. Add soy sauce and sherry, stir-fry until mixture is almost dry. Adjust seasoning with salt. Spoon into crêpes, fold bottom of crêpe over filling, fold in sides, roll up. Seal flap with a little cornstarch mixed with water. Fry in deep hot fat (375°F.) until crisp, golden brown. Makes 16 crêpes.

Spring Rolls with Shrimp and Bean Sprouts

½ pound peeled, deveined shrimp	2 tablespoons oil
1 tablespoon sherry	1 tablespoon soy sauce
1 pound bean sprouts, fresh or canned	½ teaspoon sugar
	Salt, pepper
	Cornstarch-water paste

Make Chinese Crêpes (page 26), browning them on one side only. Toss shrimp with sherry, let marinate 15 minutes, turning to season evenly. Pour boiling water over fresh bean sprouts, drain. Or, rinse and drain canned sprouts. Heat oil, add shrimp and stir-fry for a minute, until shrimp just begin to turn pink. Add sprouts, stir a minute. Add soy sauce, sugar, salt, and pepper to taste, heat. Spoon mixture onto lower half of browned side of crêpes, fold bottom over filling, fold in sides, roll up. Seal fold with a paste of cornstarch and water. Fry in deep hot fat (375°F.) until crisp and golden brown. Makes about 20 crêpes.

Scrambled Eggs with Shrimp

½ pound peeled, deveined shrimp	¼ cup oil
1 teaspoon cornstarch	6 eggs
1 teaspoon sherry	Salt
½ teaspoon finely grated ginger	

Make Chinese Crêpes (page 26), brown both sides, keep warm. Toss shrimp with cornstarch, sherry, and ginger. Heat 2 tablespoons oil and cook shrimp, stirring, until they just turn pink. Remove from pan, cool. Beat eggs, add salt to taste. Heat remaining oil in same pan, add eggs, cook, stirring, until mixture begins to thicken. Add shrimp, continue stirring until mixture is barely set. Spoon onto crêpes, fold up. Makes about 16 crêpes.

Main Dish Crêpes

Cashew Chicken Crêpes

2 cups cubed, white meat chicken	2 slices fresh ginger
1 egg white, lightly beaten	1 tablespoon sherry
Cornstarch	1 teaspoon sugar
¼ cup oil	3 tablespoons soy sauce
	1 cup salted cashew nuts

Make Chinese Crêpes (page 26), browning both sides. Keep warm. Coat chicken cubes with egg white and dredge with cornstarch. Heat oil, brown chicken and ginger slices. Discard ginger. Add sherry, sugar, soy sauce, and cashew nuts, stir-fry for a moment.

Spoon onto crêpes, using a slotted spoon; roll up. Use remaining liquid as a sauce. Makes 16 crêpes.

Red Simmered Pork Crêpes

1½ pounds pork, cut in 1-inch cubes	1 tablespoon sherry
1 cup water	½ teaspoon salt
2 slices fresh ginger root	1 teaspoon sugar
¼ cup soy sauce	2 cups fresh mushrooms, sliced

Bring pork and water to a rapid boil. Add ginger, soy sauce, sherry, and salt. Cover the pan and simmer 1 hour. Sprinkle with sugar, stir. Add mushrooms, cover, simmer 30 minutes. Make Chinese Crêpes (page 26). Keep them warm. Spoon mixture into crêpes, roll up. Makes 16 crêpes.

Crab Meat and Sesame Crêpes

1 pound crab meat, fresh, frozen, or canned	3 tablespoons vinegar
2 cucumbers, peeled and seeded	2 tablespoons sesame oil
	1 teaspoon sugar
3 tablespoons soy sauce	Salt, pepper

Make Chinese Crêpes (page 26), keep warm. Pick over crab meat and discard shells and membranes. Cut cucumbers into very thin slices. Toss crab meat and cucumbers with remaining ingredients, adjust seasoning to taste. Simmer over low heat for a few minutes to reduce liquid. Spoon crab meat and cucumber onto hot crêpes with a slotted spoon, use remaining liquid as a sauce. Fills 12 to 16 crêpes.

Char Siew Crêpes
(Marinated Pork Crêpes)

1 pound lean pork loin	¼ cup soy sauce
1 tablespoon cornstarch	¼ cup peanut oil
2 tablespoons sugar	

Make Chinese Crêpes (page 26). Cut pork into very thin slices. Toss with cornstarch, sugar, and soy sauce. Let stand 1 hour. Heat oil, cook pork slices. Spoon pork and sauce onto hot crêpes. Fills 8 crêpes.

Chinese Vegetable Crêpes

2 tablespoons oil	1 slice fresh ginger root, minced
2 cups finely shredded cabbage	1 teaspoon cornstarch
1 small onion, chopped	½ cup water
1 can (1 pound) bean sprouts, rinsed and drained	2 tablespoons sherry
1 can (½ pound) water chestnuts, drained, sliced	1 teaspoon soy sauce

Make Chinese Crêpes (page 26), keep warm. Heat oil, cook cabbage and onion, stirring constantly, until cabbage is slightly wilted. Add bean sprouts, water chestnuts, and ginger. Stir. Mix cornstarch with water, sherry, and soy sauce, add to vegetables. Cook, stirring constantly, until sauce is hot and thickened. Spoon onto crêpes, roll up. Fills 16 crêpes.

Dessert Crêpes

Crêpes Chinoise
(Flaming Kumquat Crêpes)

1 can (about 12 ounces) kumquats	¼ cup orange juice
¼ cup butter	¼ cup tangerine- or orange-flavored liqueur
¼ cup sugar	¼ cup brandy

Make Chinese Crêpes (page 26) in advance, fold into quarters. Drain syrup from kumquats and reserve. Cut the fruit into very thin slices. Melt butter, add sugar, stir for a moment. Add kumquat syrup, orange juice, and tangerine liqueur, stir until bubbly. Taste the sauce and stir in more sugar, to taste. Add sliced kumquats, heat. Turn folded crêpes in the sauce to heat. Warm brandy in a ladle, set it aflame, and pour it blazing over the crêpes. Baste crêpes with the sauce until the flame dies. Makes 16 crêpes.

Bean Paste Crêpes

Make Chinese Crêpes (page 26), spread with Chinese bean paste, a sweet puree of red beans available in cans. Roll up cigar fashion, cut into lengths. Serve as an accompaniment to fruit desserts.

10

Frittatine
(Italian Crêpes)

Take Frittatine (page 26), the Italian crêpes, add imbotte or stuffing to Italian taste. Then invite other conoscitori of fine Italian foods, and enjoy an evening made easier because you have wrapped up your Italian specialties for appetizer, main dish, or dessert. Or invite your guests for an Italian wine and Frittatine tasting, or an espresso party with dessert Frittatine. Then raise the linguist's question of the evening: Should these be called *crespelles,* an alternate name for Italian crêpes?

Appetizer Crêpe

Ham Stack

½ pound cooked ham, finely   1 clove garlic, crushed
  shredded   2 tablespoons oil
½ cup mayonnaise

Make 12 large Frittatine (page 26), keep warm. Blend ham, mayonnaise, and garlic. Stack crêpes on a buttered baking dish, spreading each with some of the ham mixture. Sprinkle top crêpe with oil, bake in moderate oven (350°F.) about 30 minutes until filling is set and crêpes are hot. Cut into pie-shaped wedges to serve. Makes hors d'oeuvre for 8 to 12.

Antipasto Crêpes

Pimiento and Anchovy Crêpes

Make Frittatine (page 26), cut in half, keep warm. On one-quarter of each crêpe arrange a well-drained pimiento or roasted Italian pepper. Top with well-drained anchovy. Fold crêpe into triangles.

Olive Condite

Fill half Frittatine with well-drained olive condite—Italian olive salad obtainable in jars.

Quick Caponata Crêpes

Fill half Frittatine with caponata—prepared eggplant relish obtainable in cans. Fold into triangles.

Artichoke Crêpes

Put a pickled artichoke heart, from a jar, on each half Frittatine. Fold into triangles.

Prosciutto Crêpes

Put a slice of honeydew or cantaloupe on the half Frittatine, top with a thin slice of prosciutto or other ham, or dried beef.

Tomato Cheese Frittatine

¾ cup chopped onion   2 egg yolks
¼ cup oil   ¼ cup grated Parmesan
2 cups Italian-style canned   cheese
  tomatoes, drained   Salt, pepper, cayenne

Prepare Frittatine (page 26), fold into quarters. Cook onion in oil until golden. Add tomatoes and simmer, stirring often, until the mixture is very thick. Cool. Add egg yolks, cheese, and salt and peppers to taste. Spoon mixture into pockets of folded crêpes. Arrange side by side on a buttered baking dish, bake in a hot oven (400°F.) about 10 minutes, until cheese melts and crêpes are hot. Makes 16.

Pizza and Cheese Frittatine

1 jar (18 ounces) prepared   Salt, pepper, oregano, garlic
  spaghetti sauce   powder
½ pound mozzarella cheese,   Optional: Slices of pepperoni,
  shredded   canned mushrooms, left-
½ cup grated Romano   over meatballs (sliced)
  cheese

Prepare Frittatine (page 26). On a cookie sheet, stack 2 or 3 leftover Italian crêpes, spoon spaghetti sauce over surface of Frittatine stack, sprinkle cheese equally over each "pie." Season to taste with spices. Garnish to taste with pepperoni, mushrooms, or meatballs. Place in moderate oven (350°F.) for 10 to 15 minutes, until cheese melts. Makes 4 to 6 "pies."

Main Dish Crêpes

Crespolini
(Italian Spinach and Cheese Crêpes)

½ cup cooked spinach,   3 tablespoons flour
  finely chopped   3½ cups milk
½ cup ricotta cheese   Salt, white pepper
1 egg   4 ounces mozzarella cheese,
¾ cup grated Romano or   grated
  Parmesan cheese   2 tablespoons butter
3 tablespoons butter

Make Frittatine (page 26), turning once to brown both sides lightly. Mix spinach, ricotta cheese, egg, and ¼ cup grated Romano or Parmesan cheese, divide onto crêpes, roll. Melt butter, stir in flour, cook for a minute without browning. Add milk and cook, stirring, until sauce is thickened and smooth. Season to taste with salt and pepper. Pour the sauce into a buttered shallow oven-proof serving dish, arrange the crêpes on the sauce. Scatter grated mozzarella cheese over the pancakes, sprinkle with remaining grated Romano or Parmesan cheese, dot with butter. Bake in a moderate (350°F.) oven about 15 to 20 minutes, until brown and bubbling hot. Fills 16 Frittatine.

Variation: Substitute for first three ingredients: 1 cup ground cooked ham mixed with 1 egg, a pinch of nutmeg, and ½ cup of the Romano cheese. Proceed as directed, sprinkle with remaining Romano, dot with butter, bake until casserole is hot and topping browns.

Turkey Frittatine Marsala

½ cooked turkey breast, sliced thin	12 thin slices cooked ham
Flour	1 can (1 pound) sliced mushrooms, drained
Salt, pepper	Parmesan cheese
Oil for frying	½ cup Marsala

Prepare Frittatine (page 26). Dust turkey slices with flour, salt, and pepper, brown delicately on both sides in oil. Remove the turkey, reserve the pan. Put cooked turkey on one-quarter of each crêpe. Cover with a slice of ham, some of the mushrooms, and a generous dusting of Parmesan cheese. Fold the crêpes in half over the filling. Arrange on a buttered baking dish. Add Marsala to the pan in which the turkey fillets were browned. Heat, scraping up browned bits, until sauce is slightly thickened, pour over the filled crêpes. Bake in a hot oven (425°F.) until the crêpes are hot and the cheese filling melted. Makes 12 Frittatine.

Frittatine Caponata
(Crêpes with Eggplant Relish Filling)

1 medium onion, sliced	1 teaspoon salt
1 stalk celery, sliced	½ teaspoon pepper
¼ cup olive oil	1 teaspoon dry basil
2 small eggplants, cut in ½-inch cubes	2 tablespoons tomato paste
3 tomatoes, peeled, seeded, and chopped	¼ cup capers
	¾ cup pitted green olives, sliced

Prepare Frittatine (page 26). Sauté onions and celery in oil until golden. Add eggplant and tomatoes and cook, uncovered, until vegetables are tender. Add seasonings, tomato paste, capers, and olives, cook until liquid is absorbed (about 15 minutes). Chill, if desired. Spoon onto crêpes, roll up. Makes filling for 16 Frittatine.

Spinach Cannelloni

2 tablespoons oil	½ teaspoon poultry seasoning herbs
¼ cup finely chopped onion	Salt, pepper to taste
1 small clove garlic, minced	1 egg
1 cup drained and chopped cooked spinach	1 can (1 pound) prepared spaghetti sauce, heated
½ cup minced cooked chicken or turkey	½ cup grated Parmesan cheese
½ cup chicken bouillon	

Prepare Frittatine (page 26), very lightly browned. Heat oil, cook onion and garlic until golden. Add spinach, chicken (or turkey), bouillon, and seasonings. Simmer over low heat for 15 minutes, covered. Remove pan from heat, beat in egg. Cool mixture before filling crêpes. Roll crêpes, arrange side by side on a buttered baking dish. Cover with spaghetti sauce, sprinkle with grated Parmesan cheese. Bake in a very hot oven (450°F.) until the topping browns and the sauce is bubbling hot. Makes filling for 8 Frittatine.

Quick Shrimp Marinara Crêpes

1 pound peeled and deveined frozen shrimp	½ onion
1 tablespoon oil	½ green pepper, slivered
1 garlic clove, crushed	1 cup (half a 1-pound jar) marinara spaghetti sauce

Make Frittatine (page 26), keep warm. Cook shrimp in oil with garlic, onion, and green pepper, until shrimp is just pink. Add sauce (reserve remainder of sauce for another use), heat. Spoon shrimp and a little sauce onto each crêpe, roll up. Top with more sauce, serve hot. Fills 12 Frittatine.

Ham Cannelloni

1 cup ground cooked ham	3 tablespoons flour
1 egg	3½ cups milk
½ cup grated Romano cheese	Salt, white pepper
Pinch of nutmeg	¼ cup grated Parmesan cheese
Salt, pepper	¼ pound Swiss cheese, shredded
¼ cup butter	

Prepare Frittatine (page 26), turning once to brown both sides lightly. Mix ham, egg, cheese, and nutmeg. Add salt and pepper to taste. Divide mixture onto crêpes, roll up. Melt butter, stir in flour, and cook for a moment, stirring. Add milk gradually and cook, stirring constantly, until the sauce is thickened and smooth. Pour the sauce into a shallow buttered baking dish. Arrange the crêpes on the sauce, sprinkle with Parmesan and Swiss cheese. Heat well in a moderate oven (350°F.), about 15 to 20 minutes. Fills 8 Frittatine.

Green Pepper Frittatine Piedmontese

4 green peppers	16 fillets of anchovy, rinsed and drained
2 cloves garlic, thinly sliced	¼ cup olive oil
2 ripe tomatoes, peeled, seeded, sliced	Salt, pepper

Prepare Frittatine (page 26). Cut green peppers into quarters, discard seeds and pith. Fill each with garlic slices and tomatoes, top with an anchovy fillet, sprinkle with olive oil, salt and pepper to taste. Arrange on an oiled baking dish, bake in a moderate oven (350°F.) about 30 minutes, until peppers are tender but still firm. (Make Frittatine while peppers are baking, or reheat them.) Fold in quarters, insert pepper in pocket, serve hot. Makes 16 Frittatine.

Cannelloni Casa Grande

1½ pounds ricotta cheese
½ pound mozzarella, shredded
3 egg yolks
Salt, pepper

1 jar (1 pound) prepared spaghetti sauce, heated
¼ cup grated Parmesan cheese

Prepare Frittatine (page 26), very lightly browned on both sides. Mix ricotta, mozzarella, and egg yolks. Season to taste with salt and pepper. Divide onto center of crêpes, roll lengthwise to encase filling. Arrange flap side down on a buttered shallow baking dish, cover with sauce, sprinkle with grated Parmesan cheese. Bake in a hot oven (400°F.) about 10 minutes, until the topping is browned and the sauce is bubbling hot. Fills 16 Frittatine.

Dessert Crêpes

Crêpes Marmellata

1 cup very thick marmalade, or apricot or other preserves
½ cup ground walnut meats or other nuts

6 tablespoons cocoa
¼ cup superfine sugar
⅛ teaspoon cinnamon or ground cloves
1 tablespoon brandy

Prepare Frittatine (page 26). Keep warm. Mix marmalade with remaining ingredients to make a thick paste. Spread on crêpes, roll up cigar fashion. Makes 16 crêpes.

Frittatine with Zabaglione

4 egg yolks
4 tablespoons sugar

4 tablespoons Marsala

Make Frittatine (page 26), fold into quarters, keep warm. Combine egg yolks and sugar in a thick-bottomed saucepan, off the heat. Beat with a sauce whisk or rotary beater until very pale and frothy. Stir in Marsala, put the pan over low heat, and cook the custard, beating constantly, until it thickens. Do not allow it to boil. Serve warm, poured over folded crêpes. Makes 16 Frittatine.

Ricotta Crêpes

½ pound ricotta
¼ cup grated milk chocolate
¼ cup finely chopped candied fruit

2 tablespoons heavy cream

Prepare Frittatine (page 26). Mix ingredients, adding more cream, if necessary, to make a light and fluffy mixture that will hold its shape. Spoon onto warm or cooled crêpes, roll up. Fills 12 crêpes.

Chestnut Cream Frittatine

¾ pound chestnuts
1½ cups milk
½ cup confectioners' sugar
½ cup heavy cream, whipped

1 tablespoon brandy
Powdered sugar

Make Frittatine (page 26), keep warm or let cool. Slit chestnuts with a cross on pointed end, cover with water, bring to a boil, and cook for 15 minutes. Cool the nuts until they can be handled. Peel off shells and inner skins. Cover the peeled nuts with milk, bring to a boil, lower the heat, simmer about 30 minutes until nuts are very soft and milk is almost absorbed. Drain excess milk, if any has not been absorbed by the chestnuts. Mash the nuts or force them through a food mill. Add enough milk to make a thick paste. Add sugar. Cool. Fold in whipped cream and brandy. Spoon mixture onto crêpes, roll up. Dust with powdered sugar. Fills 12 Frittatine.

Frittatine Imbottite con Formaggio (Stuffed Cheese Pancakes)

2 ounces Swiss cheese, grated
⅔ cup grated Parmesan cheese
1 egg, beaten

¾ cup half-and-half or light cream
Pepper, nutmeg

Prepare 10 large Frittatine (page 26), turn once to brown both sides. Mix Swiss cheese, ⅓ cup Parmesan, egg, and ¼ cup half-and-half; season to taste with pepper and nutmeg. Divide onto crêpes, roll up. Arrange stuffed crêpes side by side in a buttered shallow baking dish. Add remaining cream, sprinkle with remaining Parmesan. Bake in a moderate oven (350°F.) 15 to 20 minutes until brown and bubbling hot. Fills 10 Frittatine.

11
Blintzes

Blintzes (page 26) begin as crêpes made with a batter that is economical, easy to make, easy to use, suited to a wide variety of fillings. It is a matter of pride with accomplished Blintz makers to transform a given quantity of batter into as many thin but sturdy crêpes as possible. The crêpes—they may number from 12 to 20, depending on the skill of the maker— are baked on one side only. The browned side of the crêpe becomes the inside of the Blintz. The filling is spooned on generously and the crêpe is folded securely into a plump envelope. Finally, the envelope is browned, generally in butter, to golden crispness on both sides and served piping hot, as hors d'oeuvre, main course, or dessert. When meat or poultry is substituted for the more usual cheese or fruit fillings, water takes the place of the milk in the batter and oil or other fat is used instead of butter for the final browning.

Appetizer Crêpes

Savory Cheese Blintzes

1 pound dry pot cheese or cottage cheese	¼ cup butter
1 egg	2 tablespoons sour cream
1½ cups diced green onions	Salt, pepper

Make Blintzes (page 26), browning one side only. Turn Blintzes out on brown paper or a towel, browned side up. Mix cheese with egg. Cook onions in butter until golden, add with sour cream to cheese. Season with salt and pepper to taste. Spoon mixture on browned side of Blintzes, fold in sides, roll up to make envelopes. Just before serving, brown on both sides in butter. Fills about 8 to 10 Blintzes.

Mushrooms in Sour Cream Blintzes

2 tablespoons butter	1 teaspoon paprika
1 large onion, diced	Salt, pepper
2 cans (6 ounces each) sliced mushrooms, drained	1 cup sour cream, approximately

Make Blintzes (page 26), keep warm. Melt butter, cook onion until golden brown. Add mushrooms and seasonings, cook for a minute. Stir in enough sour cream to make a mixture that will hold its shape. Heat without boiling. Spoon onto hot Blintzes. Roll up, serve with more sour cream. Fills 12 Blintzes.

Chopped Liver Blintzes

4 chicken livers	4 hard-cooked eggs, chopped
1 large onion, minced	Salt, pepper
2 tablespoons chicken fat	

Make Blintzes (page 26), using water instead of milk. Brown both sides, keep warm. Cook livers and onion in fat until liver is just cooked through and onions are translucent. Chop finely or whirl to a smooth puree in the blender. Mix with hard-cooked eggs and season well with salt and pepper. Add a little more fat, if necessary, to make a spreadable mixture. Spread on warm crêpes, roll up cigar fashion, cut into quarters. Fills 8 Blintzes.

Herring Blintzes

Make Blintzes (page 26) just before serving. Drain most of the liquid from a 1-pound jar of herring pieces in sour cream, reserve. Chop the onions and · herring coarsely. Spoon mixture onto hot crêpes, roll up, top with reserved liquid. Fills 12 Blintzes.

Main Dish Crêpes

Grandma's Cheese Blintzes

1½ pounds dry cottage cheese	1 tablespoon sugar
1 whole egg or 2 yolks	½ teaspoon salt
½ teaspoon grated lemon rind	Garnish options: cinnamon, sugar

Make Blintzes (page 26), brown on one side only, and turn out on brown paper or a towel, browned side up. Mix cottage cheese with remaining ingredients, adjusting seasoning to suit your taste. Spoon onto browned side of Blintzes, fold in the sides, and roll up envelope style. Just before serving, brown the Blintzes on both sides in butter. Serve with sour cream and fruit preserves or fresh fruit. Or, simply sprinkle with cinnamon sugar. Fills about 12 to 16 Blintzes.

Kasha Blintzes

1 cup buckwheat groats (kasha)	½ teaspoon salt
1 egg	½ teaspoon paprika
	2 cups boiling water

Cook Blintzes (page 26) on one side; turn out browned side up on brown paper or a towel. Mix buckwheat and egg in a skillet and cook, stirring constantly with a fork, until the separate buckwheat grains are coated with egg. Meanwhile, bring 2 cups water to a boil with salt and paprika. Stir buckwheat into water, cover pan tightly, and cook until tender, about 30 minutes. Add more water, if necessary, to prevent burning. Center a spoonful of kasha on the browned side of Blintzes, fold the sides in, roll to make an envelope. Just before serving, brown on both sides in butter. Makes 8 Blintzes.

Potato Blintzes

½ cup chopped onions	1 egg yolk
3 tablespoons butter	Salt, pepper
1 cup mashed potatoes	

Blintzes (page 26) may be made in advance. Brown on one side only, turn out on brown paper or towel, browned side up. Cook onions in butter until golden. Add 1 cup mashed potatoes (fresh-cooked or instant) and blend well. Beat in egg yolk and season highly with salt and pepper. Spoon onto browned side of Blintzes, roll up, arrange on buttered baking dish. Bake in a moderate oven (350°F.) about 15 minutes, until hot. Makes 8 to 10 Blintzes.

Sour Cream Blintzes

¼ cup butter
6 tablespoons sugar
3 eggs, beaten
6 tablespoons sour cream
½ tablespoon fine white
  bread crumbs

1 tablespoon raisins
¾ cup sour cream
3 egg yolks

Blintzes (page 26), may be made in advance, as convenient. Cream butter with sugar, add eggs and 6 tablespoons sour cream. Beat well. Add bread crumbs and raisins. Fill crêpes, roll up, arrange on a buttered shallow baking dish. Blend ¾ cup sour cream with 3 egg yolks, pour over rolls. Bake in a moderate oven (350°F.) about 30 minutes. Makes 12 Blintzes.

Dessert Crêpes

Apple Meringue Blintzes

1 egg white
Dash salt
¼ cup sugar

2 medium apples, peeled,
  cored, chopped (1½ cups)
4 tablespoons brown sugar
2 tablespoons butter, melted

Brown Blintzes (page 26) on one side only. Turn out brown side up on brown paper or clean towel. Beat egg white with salt until soft peaks form when beater is withdrawn. Gradually beat in sugar, continue to beat until mixture forms stiff peaks. Fold in apples. Spoon mixture onto upper-right-hand quarter of browned side of Blintzes, fold bottom over the filling, fold left. Arrange on a shallow buttered baking dish, sprinkle with brown sugar and melted butter. Bake in a hot oven (400°F.) about 20 minutes. Makes 12 to 16 Blintzes.

Blueberry Blintzes

1½ cups blueberries, fresh
  or frozen, thawed
1 tablespoon cornstarch

1 teaspoon grated lemon rind
3 tablespoons sugar (to taste)
Cinnamon, nutmeg

Brown Blintzes (page 26) on one side only. Turn out, browned side up, on brown paper or a towel. Mix blueberries with cornstarch and lemon rind, add sugar and spices to taste. Spoon onto browned side of Blintzes; fold in sides, fold up envelope style. Just before serving, brown on both sides in butter. Makes 18 to 20 Blintzes.

Cherry Blintzes

1 can (about 1 pound) pitted
  sour cherries, water packed
1½ tablespoons flour

Ground cloves
Cinnamon
Sugar

Make Blintzes (page 26), browning them on one side only. Turn out, browned side up, on brown paper or a towel. Drain cherries well, toss with flour and spices and sugar to taste. Spoon onto browned side of crêpes. Turn sides in, roll up to make an envelope. Just before serving, brown on both sides in butter. Serve with sour cream or whipped cream. Makes 16 Blintzes.

Rich Cheese Blintzes

8 ounces (1 cup) creamed
  cottage cheese
8 ounces cream cheese,
  softened
2 egg yolks
2 tablespoons sugar

½ teaspoon grated lemon
  peel
1 teaspoon lemon juice
  (approximately)
Salt

Make Blintzes (page 26), browning them on one side. Turn them out, browned side up, on brown paper or towel. Blend cottage cheese, cream cheese, and egg yolks with sugar and lemon peel. Add lemon juice and salt to taste. Spoon onto Blintzes, fold sides over, roll up envelope style. Just before serving, brown on both sides in butter. Serve with sour cream. Makes 10 to 12 Blintzes.

Cranberry Blintzes

½ can (1 cup) whole-berry
  cranberry sauce
½ pound dry cottage cheese

Butter for frying
Sour cream

Make Blintzes (page 26), browning on one side only. Turn out on a towel, browned side up. Mix cranberry sauce and cottage cheese, spoon mixture onto browned side of Blintzes. Fold bottom over filling, fold in sides, roll up. Melt butter, cook Blintzes until brown on both sides, seam side first. Serve with sour cream. Fills 12 to 16.

12

Palacsinta
(Hungarian Pancakes)

Hungary's Palacsinta (page 26), called Palatschinken in the German-speaking countries of crêpe-loving Mittel-Europa, are among the most delicate of crêpes, tender and fluffy with beaten egg white, crisp because they are slightly lower in fat than usual. Fillings for Palacsinta tend to the luxurious and rich—the best deserves the best. Yet, in the European tradition, these crêpes can be used to make much of small amounts of food. They are also most practical to serve. Palacsinta are generally filled, rolled, and placed in a casserole with a topping of sour cream, butter, and sugar or other sauce, and baked to reheat. The initial preparation may be done ahead of serving, an asset for the cook.

Main Dish Crêpes

Fish and Tomato Salad Palacsinta

½ pound boneless cooked
  or smoked fish, cubed
2 medium cooked potatoes,
  diced
1 large dill pickle, chopped
  coarsely
⅔ cup mayonnaise

1 tablespoon vinegar
4 green onions (scallions)
  sliced thin
1 teaspoon paprika
Salt and pepper to taste
2 tomatoes, sliced thin

Make Palacsinta (page 26). Combine fish and potatoes with pickles, mayonnaise, vinegar, onions,
paprika, salt, and pepper. Mix well. Place two overlapping tomato slices on each crêpe, top with fish
salad, and roll up. Refrigerate until ready to serve.
Makes 4 servings.

Fish in Sharp Sauce Palacsinta

1 pound boneless fish, in
  strips
Flour for dredging
6 tablespoons butter
1 small onion, chopped
1 clove garlic, minced
1 green pepper, chopped

1 tomato, peeled, seeded, and
  chopped
Salt and pepper to taste
2 teaspoons paprika
2 tablespoons vinegar
1 teaspoon dry mustard
½ cup sour cream

Make Palacsinta (page 26). Dredge fish pieces in
flour, brown lightly in hot butter, remove from pan.
In the same pan, sauté onions, garlic, and green
peppers until tender. Stir in remaining ingredients
except for sour cream and cook, stirring frequently,
until thickened. Remove from heat and blend in sour
cream. Arrange fish pieces on crêpes, top with sauce,
and roll up. Arrange seam side down in a buttered
baking dish and bake in a moderate oven (375°F.)
for 10 minutes, until hot. Makes 4 servings.

Paprikash Crêpes

2 tablespoons butter
1 pound veal for stew, in
  cubes
1 small onion, diced

Salt, pepper
2 teaspoons paprika
¼ cup water, as needed
1 cup sour cream

Make Palacsinta (page 26). Melt butter and cook
veal and onion until onion is golden. Add salt, pepper, and paprika. Cook, stirring often, until meat is
brown. Cover the pan, simmer until meat is tender,
about 40 minutes. Add a little water as needed to
prevent burning. Add ½ cup sour cream, heat without boiling. Spoon onto hot crêpes, roll, arrange on
a buttered shallow baking dish. Brush crêpes with
remaining sour cream, bake in a moderate oven
(350°F.) until hot. Makes 4 to 6 servings.

Kaposztaspalacsinta
(Hungarian Cabbage Pancakes)

1 cup finely shredded
  cabbage

2 tablespoons butter
Salt, pepper

Make the batter for Palacsinta (page 26). Cook
cabbage in butter, covered, until just tender. Season
with salt and pepper to taste. Add to crêpe batter.
Make crêpes; the cakes will be thicker than usual.
Serve hot. *Variation:* Sprinkle a little chopped ham
on the crêpes. Makes 18 to 24 crêpes.

Veal Goulash Palacsinta

1 pound veal, cut into ¾-
  inch cubes
4 tablespoons oil
1 large onion, chopped
1 green pepper, chopped
2 tomatoes, peeled, seeded,
  and chopped
1 large potato, in ½-inch
  cubes

1 clove garlic, minced
Salt and pepper to taste
⅛ teaspoon cumin
1 tablespoon paprika
Water
3 tablespoons butter

Make Palacsinta (page 26). Cook meat in hot oil until lightly browned. Add onions, peppers, and tomatoes, and cook, stirring frequently, until vegetables
are wilted. Stir in potatoes and seasonings and enough
water barely to cover. Continue cooking, uncovered, until meat and potatoes are cooked. Spoon
mixture onto crêpes and roll up. Arrange seam side
down in a shallow baking dish, dot with butter, and
sprinkle with more paprika. Bake in a hot oven
(400°F.) 15 minutes, or until filling is very hot.
Makes 4 to 6 servings.

Topfelpalatschinken
(German Cottage Cheese Crêpes)

½ cup butter
¾ cup sugar
3 eggs
1 cup (½ pound) cottage
  cheese
½ cup raisins
½ cup sour cream

½ teaspoon salt
1 teaspoon vanilla
Grated rind of 1 lemon
2 cups milk
2 eggs
⅔ cup sugar

Make Palacsinta (page 26). Cream butter with ¾
cup sugar. Add 3 eggs, one at a time, beating well
after each. Drain cottage cheese well, add to butter
mixture with raisins and sour cream. Add salt, vanilla, and lemon rind. Spread crêpes with cheese
mixture, arrange side by side in a buttered baking
dish. Beat milk with 2 eggs and ⅔ cup sugar, pour
over filled crêpes, bake in a moderate oven (350°F.)
about 25 minutes. Serve hot. Makes 4 servings.

Dessert Crêpes

Crêpes Gundel
(Hungarian-Style Dessert Pancakes)

½ cup walnuts, finely ground Grated zest of a small
¼ cup rum   orange
½ cup sugar   Butter
4 tablespoons softened butter 1 cup Chocolate Sauce (page
Milk to make a paste   79), flavored with 1 table-
¼ cup sultana raisins   spoon rum

Make Palacsinta (page 26). Combine walnuts, rum, sugar and butter in a blender, and whirl to a smooth paste, adding milk as required. Or pound the nuts in a mortar and combine with other ingredients. Stir in raisins and orange zest. Spoon onto crêpes and roll up. Arrange seam side down in a buttered baking dish and bake in a moderate oven (350°F.) 10 minutes, until hot. Cover with chocolate sauce and serve immediately. Makes 5 or more servings.

Whipped Apricot Cream Palacsinta

1 envelope unflavored gelatin 1 cup apricot preserves
¼ cup water   ½ teaspoon vanilla
3 eggs, separated   1 teaspoon lemon juice
⅓ cup sugar   ½ cup cream, whipped
1 cup scalded milk

Make Palacsinta (page 26). Soften gelatin in water. Beat egg yolks with sugar and slowly add milk. Add gelatin, stir until dissolved. Cook over hot water, stirring constantly, until mixture thickens. Cool, add apricot preserves, vanilla, and lemon juice. Beat egg whites until stiff but not dry, fold in whipped cream. Fold both into the egg-yolk mixture. Spoon onto crêpes and roll up. Refrigerate at least 2 hours before serving. Fills about 20 crêpes.

Dessert Palacsinta Hungarian
(Dessert Pancakes Hungarian Style)

¾ cup grated nuts   1 cup semisweet chocolate
2 tablespoons white raisins   pieces (6 oz.)
2 tablespoons sugar   1 cup jam

Prepare Palacsinta (page 26). Combine grated nuts with the sugar and white raisins. Melt the chocolate over hot water, smooth. Arrange the pancakes in layers in an oven-proof dish, with different fillings between the layers. Use nuts on the first, chocolate on the second, and jam on the third. Top with a last layer of pancakes. Keep hot in the oven, with the door open, until ready to serve. Serve with Wine Sauce (below). Makes 5 stacks. Cut each stack in half for 10 servings.

Wine Sauce

4 egg yolks   1 cup dry white wine
Dash flour   1 stick cinnamon
4 tablespoons sugar   1 or 2 cloves
Few drops vanilla

Beat the egg yolks with the flour, sugar, and vanilla until light, beat in remaining ingredients. Chill until serving time. Strain out the spices and cook the sauce over very low heat, beating constantly with a whisk until it is thickened and frothy. Serve hot with Palacsinta. Makes 1½ cups.

Light Cheese Palacsinta

1 cup cottage or ricotta   3 eggs, separated
   cheese   3 tablespoons sugar
⅓ cup white raisins   Dash cinnamon
2 tablespoons yogurt   ½ cup butter, melted

Prepare Palacsinta (page 26). Mix cottage cheese with raisins, yogurt, egg yolks, sugar, cinnamon, and ¼ cup butter. Beat egg whites stiff, fold in. Fill crêpes, roll up, arrange in a buttered shallow baking dish. This can be done in advance. Pour remaining butter over the crêpes. Bake in a moderately hot oven (375°F.) about 30 minutes, until crêpes and filling are very hot. Makes about 16.

13

Plättar

(Swedish Pancakes)

The very light Swedish pancakes, called Plättar (page 26), are generally made in a pan with shallow, small, round sections for individual pancakes, the batter thinner and more runny than that for a French crêpe. If you do not have a Plättar pan, drop batter by tablespoons onto a very hot griddle, and fry on both sides until nicely browned. Traditional Swedish Thursday dinner includes yellow pea soup with pork, followed by Plättar with lingonberry preserves. A variety of Scandinavian pancake fillings are included here, for any day of the week.

Appetizer Crêpes

Plättar Stockholm

6 ounces smoked salmon,   **2 tablespoons butter, melted**
shredded   **¼ cup fresh bread crumbs**
4 hard-cooked eggs, chopped
1 tablespoon minced fresh
dillweed

Make Plättar (page 26). Mix smoked salmon, eggs, and dill. Spoon onto Plättar, fold in sides, fold over. Arrange, seam side down, on a shallow buttered baking dish. Sprinkle with butter, scatter with bread crumbs. Bake in a hot oven (400°F.) until crumbs are toasted and browned. Makes about 20 Plättar.

Dessert Crêpes

Pannkakor med Sylt
(Pancakes with Jam)

1 jar (about 1 pound) lingon-   **1 cup heavy cream, whipped**
berry preserves

Make Plättar (page 26). Place on very hot platter and serve immediately with lingonberries and whipped cream. The lingonberries are generally passed in a clear glass sauceboat, the cream in a separate bowl. Makes 6 to 8 servings.

Cranberry Sauce for Plättar

Cranberries are a satisfactory substitute for the Scandinavian lingonberries, base of a favorite sauce to serve with Plättar.

1 quart cranberries   **2 cups water**
2 cups sugar

Make Plättar (page 26) just before serving, if possible. Wash berries, discard stems. Combine in saucepan with sugar and water, boil rapidly until berries pop open, 5 minutes. Serve warm or cooled with hot Plättar. Top with whipped cream or cream cheese whipped with a little milk. Chill remaining cranberry sauce for other uses. Makes 1 quart.

Scandinavian Rhubarb Plättar

2 pounds rhubarb   **1 teaspoon vanilla extract**
⅔ cup sugar   **¼ cup cornstarch**

Make Plättar (page 26) just before serving, if possible. Peel rhubarb, if necessary (young, tender pink stalks do not need peeling), cut it into ½-inch lengths. Add sugar and water barely to cover, simmer until rhubarb is very tender. Add vanilla and more sugar to taste. Stir cornstarch with a little water, add to hot rhubarb, cook until clear and thickened. Spoon over hot or reheated Plättar on serving plates. Chill remaining rhubarb for other uses. Makes 6 to 8 servings.

Plättar with Applesauce Whip

1 envelope unflavored gelatin   **2 tablespoons lemon juice**
½ cup cold water   **¼ cup sugar**
1 jar (1 pound) applesauce   **3 ice cubes**
or 2 cups homemade

Make Plättar (page 26) just before serving, if possible. Sprinkle gelatin on cold water to soften. Stir over medium heat until gelatin dissolves. Add applesauce, lemon juice, and sugar to taste, and stir to dissolve sugar. Add ice cubes, stir until ice melts. Beat with a rotary beater until mixture is light and fluffy. Pile onto freshly made or reheated Plättar, serve at once. Makes about 6 servings.

14

Blini
(Russian Pancakes)

The distinctive flavor of Blini (page 26), those hearty yet delicate pancakes of Russia, comes from the buckwheat flour used in the batter. For the expatriate or the devoted reader of Russian novels, hot Blini crowned with caviar from an ice-jacketed bowl, set off with chopped egg, the sharp bite of onion, and the smoothness of sour cream, nostalgically evoke memories of gala parties, romance, motherland. Blini with hearty fillings make a supper or buffet dish of distinction. Sweetly filled blini make delightful desserts or snacks to serve with tea.

Appetizer Crêpes

Caviar and Accoutrements for Blini

3 ounces caviar
4 hard-cooked eggs, whites
  and yolks separated and
  chopped
1 small onion, sliced into
  thin rings

½ pound sweet butter,
  shaped into curls
1 cup sour cream

Make small Blini (page 26), keep warm. Spoon the caviar into a glass dish and set the dish into a larger glass bowl filled with cracked ice. Surround serving bowl with separate dishes holding chopped egg yolk, chopped egg white, onion rings, butter curls, and sour cream. Pass very hot Blini; invite guests to spread each Blini with butter, add a small mound of caviar and top with egg white, egg yolk, onion, and a dollop of sour cream. If desired, serve with iced vodka or champagne. Makes 16 Blini.

Smoked Salmon and Whipped Cream Cheese for Blini

½ pound cream cheese at
  room temperature
¼ cup heavy cream,
  whipped

½ pound thinly sliced
  smoked Nova Scotia
  salmon

Make small Blini (page 26), keep warm. Beat the cream cheese with a rotary beater until fluffy. Fold in the whipped cream. Arrange the salmon on a serving plate. Invite guests to top Blini with cream cheese mixture and salmon. Makes 8 servings.

Creamed Herring and Blini

1 pound pickled herring
1 cup thick sour cream
3 tablespoons lemon juice
1 large onion, sliced
1 teaspoon peppercorns

1 teaspoon salt
1 teaspoon sugar
Paprika
2 tablespoons chopped
  parsley

Make small Blini (page 26) just before serving. A day before Blini will be served, cut herring into bite-size pieces. Mix sour cream, lemon juice, onion slices, peppercorns, salt, and sugar. Pour sauce over herring and toss with a fork. Refrigerate overnight. Serve herring on a platter and sprinkle with paprika and parsley. Serve hot Blini separately. Invite guests to top Blini with herring. Makes about 8 servings.

Corned Beef Spread

1 envelope gelatin
⅓ cup cold water
1 cup hot beef broth
1 tablespoon Dijon-style
  mustard
1 tablespoon lemon juice

1 small onion, finely chopped
1 cup celery, finely chopped
¼ cup chopped parsley
2 cups finely ground corned
  beef
Sour cream

Make small Blini (page 26) just before serving. Sprinkle gelatin on cold water to soften. Combine with beef broth and bring to boil in a saucepan, stirring constantly, until gelatin is dissolved. Cool. Add remaining ingredients, except sour cream, blend thoroughly. Turn into a 4- or 5-cup mold and refrigerate overnight. Unmold to serve. Pass hot Blini and sour cream separately. Makes 16 servings.

Spiced Ham Spread for Blini
(Ham Timbales)

2 tablespoons butter
¼ cup dry bread crumbs
½ cup chicken stock or
  broth
1 cup finely ground cooked
  ham
2 tablespoons vodka or
  sherry

½ cup chopped parsley
2 eggs, beaten
Salt, freshly ground pepper
Pinch cayenne
⅛ teaspoon ground cloves
⅛ teaspoon ground mace
Sour cream

Make small Blini (page 26) just before serving. Melt butter, add bread crumbs and cook five minutes, stirring constantly. Add chicken broth, ham, vodka, parsley, and eggs. Season with salt, pepper, cayenne, cloves, and mace. Turn into a buttered 3-cup mold, set the mold in a pan of hot water, cover with foil, and bake in a moderate oven (350°F.) 20 minutes. Cool, cut into thin slices. Serve with hot Blini and sour cream, invite guests to wrap their own. Makes 16 servings.

Main Dish Crêpes

Roast Beef with Horseradish Sauce for Blini

24 very thin slices roast beef
½ cup Hollandaise Sauce
  (page 53) or mayonnaise
¼ cup heavy cream, whipped

1 teaspoon freshly grated
  horseradish or 1½ tea-
  spoons prepared, drained
  horseradish

Make large Blinis (page 26) in crêpe pan. Combine Hollandaise Sauce with whipped cream and horseradish. Place two thin slices of roast beef on each Blini, top with 1 tablespoon horseradish sauce, roll up. Fills 12 Blini.

Red Cabbage with Ham for Blini

1 red cabbage (about 2
  pounds), washed and
  shredded
1 small apple
½ pound smoked ham,
  cooked and cut in
  matchsticks

6 tablespoons butter
½ teaspoon freshly ground
  black pepper
Salt to taste
1 tablespoon prepared
  mustard

Make Blini (page 26), keep warm. Soak shredded cabbage in cold, salted water to cover for 30 minutes. Peel and dice apple, add. Bring to a boil and simmer until cabbage is just tender, still slightly crisp. Drain. Combine with ham, butter, pepper, salt, and mustard. Spoon mixture onto hot Blini, roll up. Use to fill about 16 Blini. Chill remaining cabbage mixture for other uses.

Beef Stroganoff for Blini

¼ cup oil
2 cups thinly sliced onion rings
½ pound mushrooms, sliced
1 pound beef fillet or sirloin
Salt, freshly ground black pepper
½ tablespoon dry mustard
½ tablespoon sugar
Dash Worcestershire sauce
1 cup sour cream

Make large Blini (page 26), keep warm. Heat 2 tablespoons oil in a skillet. Add onion rings and mushrooms and cook, stirring occasionally, until vegetables are tender. Season with salt and pepper. Drain off excess fat. In a second skillet, heat 2 tablespoons oil. Cut meat into ¼-by-2-inch strips. Brown strips lightly in oil about half at a time and add to vegetables. Season with mustard, sugar, and Worcestershire to taste. Add sour cream, a little at a time, and heat without boiling. Spoon mixture onto Blini, roll up. Fills 16 large Blini.

Salade Russe (Vegetable Salad)

¼ cup diced boiled pickled tongue or cooked salmon
½ cup diced cooked carrots
½ cup diced cooked beets
½ cup cooked green peas
¾ cup mayonnaise

Make large Blini (page 26) just before serving. Combine tongue or salmon, carrots, beets, and peas, gently fold in mayonnaise. Cover and chill. Spoon onto hot Blini, roll. Fills 12 Blini.

Stuffed Blini Stack

4 cups mushrooms, sliced
2 large onions, sliced
½ cup butter, softened
Salt, pepper to taste
1 hard-cooked egg, finely chopped
2 tablespoons chopped parsley
3 tablespoons sour cream
1 egg, beaten
Bread crumbs

Make Blini (page 26), browning one side only. Cook mushrooms and onions in half the butter until tender. Cool slightly, add salt and pepper, egg, parsley, and sour cream. Spread the unbrowned side of one Blini with a little butter and 2 tablespoons of filling. Cover with another Blini and repeat to make four layers. Make 3 more stacks. Brush top and sides with beaten egg, sprinkle with bread crumbs. Bake in a hot oven (425°F.) 10 to 15 minutes, until

golden brown. Serve with sour cream. Makes 4 hearty servings.

Dessert Crêpes

Maple Whipped Butter Topping

⅓ cup granulated sugar
⅓ cup maple syrup
¼ cup water
2 egg yolks
1 cup softened butter

Make Blini (page 26) just before serving. Boil sugar, maple syrup, and water to 240°F. on a candy thermometer; a little syrup will form a soft ball in cold water. Beat egg yolks until light and fluffy, gradually beat in syrup and continue beating until the mixture is cool. Add butter, bit by bit, until all is incorporated. Serve as topping for Blini. Makes about 16.

Whipped Cheese with Chocolate Sauce

CHOCOLATE SAUCE
½ cup cocoa
1 cup sugar
1 cup corn syrup
½ cup light cream
¼ teaspoon salt
4 tablespoons sweet butter
2 tablespoons kirsch or rum

WHIPPED CHEESE
½ cup heavy cream
4 tablespoons sugar
1 lb. cottage cheese

Make large Blini (page 26), keep warm. *Make sauce:* Combine cocoa, sugar, corn syrup, cream, salt, and butter in a heavy-bottomed saucepan. Cook over moderate heat, stirring constantly, until the mixture comes to the boil. Boil for 4 to 5 minutes, stirring occasionally. Remove from heat and stir in the liqueur. *Whipped Cheese:* Place cream, sugar and cottage cheese in blender container. Whirl until smooth and creamy. Top half the warm Blini with Crème Fraîche, cover with a second Blini. Pour hot Chocolate Sauce over the Blini. Makes sauce for about 30 Blini.

Raisin and Sour Cream Sauce for Blini

¾ cup seedless raisins
1 cup hot water
½ cup sugar
2 tablespoons butter
½ cup sour cream
1 tablespoon flour
Dash salt

Make large Blini (page 26); fold into quarters, keep warm. Combine raisins, water, sugar, and butter. Bring to a boil, reduce heat, and simmer for 15 minutes. Add sour cream, mixed with flour and salt. Bring just to the boiling point, stirring constantly, but do not allow sauce to boil. Spoon sauce over Blini. Makes 8 servings.

Russian Baba Blini

¼ cup dried currants   ¾ cup water
¼ cup sultana raisins   ½ cup dark rum
1 cup sugar

Make batter for Blini (page 26), adding currants and raisins to batter before rising. Meanwhile, combine sugar and water in a heavy-bottomed saucepan. Bring to a boil and cook without stirring until the mixture forms a thick syrup that coats a spoon (228°F. on a candy thermometer). Pour the syrup into a bowl and stir in the rum. Make Blini, serve hot with rum-flavored syrup. Makes 16.

Jam Custard Blini

1 cup finely ground almonds   1 egg yolk
2 teaspoons milk   ¼ cup sour cream
3 tablespoons raspberry jam   1 teaspoon cinnamon
3 tablespoons apricot jam   1 tablespoon unsalted butter

Make small Blini (page 26) or French Crêpes (page 25) or Blender Crêpes (page 25), in advance, if desired. Soak ground almonds in milk for 10 minutes. Pass jams through a strainer or food mill, add egg yolk, sour cream, cinnamon, and the nut-and-milk mixture. Spoon filling onto Blini and arrange on a greased cookie sheet. Bake in a hot oven (400°F.) for 20 minutes or until topping is set. Makes about 25.

15
Beer Crêpes

Beer in the batter is the secret of very light crêpes, a specialty of Swiss chefs. These fluffy Beer Crêpes (page 26) are ideal with flavorful German fillings, from Liptauer cheese to Tongue with Raisin Sauce to Almond Rum Crêpes. One taste, and you will understand why Beer Crêpes are the champagne-priced offering at some very expensive restaurants.

Appetizer Crêpes

Liptauer Crêpes

2 cups (1 pound) cottage cheese	2 teaspoons dry mustard
4 anchovy fillets, drained and chopped	½ teaspoon salt
	¼ teaspoon celery salt
2 teaspoons caraway seeds	2 teaspoons chopped chives
2 teaspoons paprika	2 tablespoons chopped watercress

Prepare Beer Crêpes (page 26). Force cottage cheese through a sieve, or whirl it in a blender. Add remaining ingredients, mix well. Spoon onto hot or cold crêpes, roll up. Fills 16 crêpes.

Beet and Herring Salad Crêpes

½ cup chopped pickled herring	2 hard-cooked eggs, chopped
½ cup diced boiled beets	3 tablespoons mild vinegar
½ cup diced boiled potatoes	⅓ cup oil
½ cup chopped onions	1 teaspoon sugar
	Salt, pepper

Make Beer Crêpes (page 26) just before serving, or make ahead and reheat. Combine salad ingredients, let stand at room temperature for 30 minutes to mellow. Fold crêpes into quarters, fill pockets with herring salad. Fills 16 or more crêpes.

Liver and Apple Crêpes

1 pound liver—beef, pork or chicken	2 onions, sliced thin
	2 apples, peeled, cored, sliced
Flour, salt, pepper	½ teaspoon sugar
¼ cup butter	Salt, pepper

Make Beer Crêpes (page 26), keep warm. Cut beef or pork liver into thin slices, or cut chicken livers into halves. Dust pieces with flour seasoned with salt and pepper. Melt butter, brown liver pieces on both sides, add onions, cook until onions are wilted. Add apple slices, season with a little sugar and salt and pepper to taste. Cover the pan and simmer over low heat until liver is cooked through and apples are fork tender. Spoon into crêpes, serve hot. Fills 12 to 16 crêpes.

Deviled Pineapple Crêpes

1 cup (½ pound) cottage cheese	1 tablespoon brown sugar
	½ teaspoon prepared mustard
1 can (about 4 ounces) deviled ham	½ teaspoon Worcestershire sauce
1 can (1 pound) pineapple chunks, drained	Pinch of cloves

Make Beer Crêpes (page 26), fold into quarters, keep warm. Mix cottage cheese, ham and remaining ingredients, spoon into pockets in warm crêpes. Fills 12 crêpes.

Sardine and Cheese Crêpes

3 cans (about 4 ounces each) boneless, skinless sardines in oil	2 tomatoes, sliced thin
	Salt, pepper
12 thin slices Port du Salut or favorite cheese	

Make Beer Crêpes (page 26) in advance, as convenient. Drain sardines, arrange on lower quarter of crêpes. Cover with a slice of cheese and a slice of tomato, and sprinkle with salt and pepper to taste. Fold crêpes into quarters, arrange on a buttered baking dish. Bake in a hot oven (400°F.) about 15 minutes, until crêpes are hot and cheese melted. Fills 12 crêpes.

Main Dish Crêpes

Lobster Stack Crêpes

1 can (8 ounces) mushrooms	½ cup sour cream
1 cup diced lobster meat	1 slice white bread
1 tablespoon chopped parsley	1 tablespoon melted butter
Salt, pepper	

Make Beer Crêpes (page 26) in advance, as convenient. Drain mushrooms, reserving liquid, and mix with lobster, parsley, seasonings, and sour cream. Crumble bread, soak crumbs in mushroom liquid. Drain off excess liquid, add bread to mixture. Stack crêpes in layers on a buttered baking dish, spreading each crêpe with some of the lobster filling. Sprinkle top crêpe with melted butter. Bake in a moderate oven (350°F.) about 20 minutes until filling is set and crêpes are piping hot. Cut into pie-shaped wedges. Serves 8 to 10.

Tongue and Raisin Sauce Crêpes

1 tablespoon cornstarch	¼ cup brown sugar
1 cup water	¼ cup seedless raisins
1 chicken bouillon cube	12 to 16 slices cooked tongue
¼ cup wine vinegar	

Beer Crêpes (page 26) may be made in advance. In a saucepan, mix cornstarch with water, add bouillon cube, vinegar, sugar, and raisins. Cook, stirring constantly, until sauce is slightly thickened and smooth. Warm tongue slices in the sauce. Arrange tongue and a little sauce on each crêpe, roll up. Arrange crêpes side by side in a buttered baking dish, spoon remaining sauce over the crêpes. Bake in a hot oven (400°F.) about 15 minutes, until crêpes are piping hot. Fills 12 to 16 crêpes.

Crêpes with Quick Coq au Vin

4 cups diced cooked chicken
   or turkey
1 can (8 ounces) white
   onions, drained
1 can (4 ounces) mushrooms

¾ cup red wine
1 tablespoon cornstarch
Pinch of poultry seasoning
Salt, pepper

Prepare Beer Crêpes (page 26), keep warm. Combine chicken, onions, and mushrooms, and their liquid. Stir wine with cornstarch to make a paste, add to chicken, mix. Heat slowly, stirring often. Add seasonings to taste. Spoon into warm crêpes, serve hot. Fills 16 crêpes.

Sauerkraut Goulash Crêpes

1 onion, chopped
2 tablespoons bacon fat
1 pound sauerkraut
½ teaspoon caraway seeds
1 onion, sliced
3 tablespoons bacon fat
¾ pound boneless pork
   shoulder, cut in cubes

¾ pound beef for stew, cut
   in cubes
1 cup water
1 cup sour cream
2 teaspoons paprika
Salt, pepper

Make 24 Beer Crêpes (page 26) just before serving. In a saucepan cook chopped onion in 2 tablespoons bacon fat until brown. Drain sauerkraut, reserve 1 cup juice. Add to pan with caraway seeds. Stir over low heat for a few minutes. Add reserved juice, cover, cook 30 minutes until sauerkraut is tender. Add water if necessary to prevent burning. In a stew pan cook sliced onion in 3 tablespoons bacon fat until brown. Add meat cubes, brown on all sides. Add water, cover, cook until meat is tender. Add more water, as necessary, to prevent burning. Combine meat and sauerkraut, add sour cream and seasonings to taste. Spoon the goulash into hot Beer Crêpes, serve hot. Fills 24 crêpes.

Crab-Filled Crêpes

1 can (8 ounces) crab meat
¼ cup mayonnaise
2 scallions, minced
½ green pepper, minced
2 tablespoons slivered celery

1 teaspoon mustard
Salt, pepper, cayenne
2 tablespoons butter
¼ cup grated cheese

Make Beer Crêpes (page 26). Pick over crab meat and discard shells and membranes. Mix with scallions, green pepper, celery, and mustard, season to taste with salt, pepper, and cayenne. Spread mixture on crêpes, arrange seam side down on buttered baking dish. Dot with butter, sprinkle with cheese, and bake in a hot oven (400°F.) about 15 minutes, until the cheese melts and browns. Fills 4 appetizer crêpes.

Variation: Pour over the filled crêpes 1 can condensed cream of mushroom, asparagus, celery, or shrimp soup, heated with ¼ cup cream or milk.

Broccoli Crêpes

1 package (10 ounces) frozen
   chopped broccoli
Salt, pepper
1 hard-cooked egg, sliced
1 can (10½ ounces) con-
   densed cream of asparagus or cream of celery
   soup

¼ cup milk
½ cup coarsely grated Cheddar cheese

Make Beer Crêpes (page 26). Cook broccoli until just tender, drain well, season with salt and pepper. Divide onto crêpes. Top with a slice of egg. Roll crêpes, arrange seam side down in a buttered shallow baking dish. Blend soup with milk, heat, pour over crêpes, sprinkle with cheese. Bake in a hot oven (400°F.) about 20 minutes, until the cheese browns. Fills 8 to 10 crêpes.

Variation: Substitute cooked asparagus spears, fresh or frozen, for the broccoli.

Mushroom Crêpe Stacks

2 tablespoons butter
¾ cup sliced fresh mush-
   rooms

Salt, pepper
¼ cup sour cream
1 small egg, beaten

Make Beer Crêpes (page 26). Melt butter, add mushrooms, cook until just tender. Season with salt and pepper to taste, add sour cream and half the beaten egg. Stack crêpes on a buttered baking dish, spreading each with some of the mushroom mixture. Brush the top layer with egg. Bake in a moderate oven (350°F.) until the egg topping is set. Serves 8.

Dessert Crêpes

Green Grapes and Sour Cream Crêpes

2 cups green seedless grapes
¼ cup sour cream

Brown sugar

Make Beer Crêpes (page 26). Toss grapes with sour cream and brown sugar to taste. Spoon mixture onto reheated or cold crêpes, serve for dessert, topped with more sour cream and a sprinkling of brown sugar, if desired. Fills 12 to 16 crêpes.

Almond Rum Crêpes

2 egg yolks
¾ cup confectioners' sugar
⅓ cup dark rum

1 cup heavy cream
¾ cup chopped toasted
    almonds

Prepare Beer Crêpes (page 26). Beat egg yolks and sugar until very light and creamy. Beat in rum. Whip cream stiff, fold in egg mixture. Fill crêpes, warm or cool, with the cream, sprinkle with toasted almonds. (To toast almonds spread the nuts on a baking pan, bake in a slow oven [250°F.] about 20 minutes. The almond skins may easily be removed at about the halfway point.) Fills 12 to 16 crêpes.

Lemon Butter Cream Fillings

½ cup sugar
2 tablespoons butter
Pinch salt
2 teaspoons grated lemon
    rind

3 egg yolks, slightly beaten
2 tablespoons lemon juice
½ cup heavy cream,
    whipped

Prepare Beer Crêpes (page 26). Combine sugar, butter, salt, lemon rind and slightly beaten egg yolks in small, cold saucepan. Cook over low heat, stirring constantly, until thickened. Remove from heat. Add lemon juice. Chill. Fold in whipped cream. Fill crêpes. Roll. Fills about 12 crêpes.

Magic Microwave Apple Crêpes

2 McIntosh or Rome Beauty
    apples
Juice of ½ lemon
¼ cup sugar
½ teaspoon cinnamon

3 tablespoons butter
½ cup whipped cream
1 tablespoon slivered,
    toasted almonds

Prepare Beer Crêpes (page 26). Peel apples, core and cut into thin wedges. Drop into lemon juice with cold water to cover, to prevent discoloration. Combine sugar and cinnamon. Drain apples, toss with cinnamon sugar. Divide onto crêpes. Dot apples with butter. Roll crêpes, place on serving plate, seam down. Microwave heat about 2 minutes or until apples are soft. Top with whipped cream and toasted almonds. Makes 2 servings.

Honey Almond Filling

⅓ cup butter
½ cup honey
½ cup sugar
½ teaspoon salt

½ teaspoon cinnamon
½ cup toasted chopped
    almonds

Prepare Beer Crêpes (page 26). Combine butter, honey, sugar, salt and cinnamon in saucepan. Bring to boil over low heat, stirring constantly. Boil 2 minutes, remove from heat. Beat vigorously until very thick and taffy-like; fold in almonds. If too stiff to spread, heat again. Fill crêpes. Roll. Makes filling for about 12 crêpes.

16
Eggnog Crêpes

You will want to toast Eggnog Crêpes (page 26), made with leftover or prepared eggnog in the batter. They are extra rich and flavorful, and set off fillings that are simple to prepare, but give any day a holiday feeling. No eggnog? Use the fillings which follow for Palacsinta (page 26) or Classic French Crêpes (page 25) or Quick Crêpes (page 25). Add an extra egg and a little rum to the crêpe batter, for an "eggnog" flavor.

Dessert Crêpes

Banana Crêpes

8 small firm bananas   ¼ cup brown sugar
¼ cup butter   2 tablespoons rum

Make Eggnog Crêpes (page 26), keep warm. Peel bananas and cut them in half. Melt butter in a skillet, add sugar and rum, stir until sugar is melted. Add bananas, cover, cook about 5 minutes, turning once. Put a banana half on each crêpe, roll up, top with sauce. Makes 16 crêpes.

Mincemeat Crêpes

1 jar (1 pound) mincemeat   Confectioners' sugar
1 tart apple, peeled and
  chopped

Make Eggnog Crêpes (page 26). Mix mincemeat with apple, spoon on crêpes, roll up. Dust with confectioners' sugar, put under broiler, heat for a moment to glaze. Makes 16 crêpes.

Cherries Jubilee Crêpes

1 can (1 pound 14 ounces)   ½ teaspoon cinnamon
  bing cherries   ¼ cup brandy

Make Eggnog Crêpes (page 26), browning both sides, fold into quarters. Drain the syrup from the cherries into a saucepan, or into the top pan of a chafing dish. Boil rapidly until the juice is reduced to half its original volume. Add cinnamon and cherries, heat. Add quartered crêpes, turn to heat and coat both sides with sauce. Warm brandy in a ladle, ignite it, pour flaming into the pan. Baste crêpes with sauce until flame dies. Makes 6 to 8 servings.

Rum Whipped Cream Crêpes

1 cup heavy cream   2 tablespoons dark rum
2 tablespoons confectioners'
  sugar

Make Eggnog Crêpes (page 26), turning once to brown both sides. Whip cream until it is thick; stir in sugar and rum. Use to fill crêpes, hot or cooled. Makes 16 crêpes.

Variations: Flavor whipped cream to your own taste with sugar and brandy or a fruit liqueur.

Bourbon Apple Raisin Crêpes

2 cups chopped fresh apples   ½ teaspoon cinnamon
¼ cup raisins   Pinch salt
¼ cup butter   2 tablespoons Bourbon
½ cup brown sugar   ¼ cup chopped nuts

Make Eggnog Crêpes (page 26), turning once to brown both sides. Keep warm. Cook apples and raisins in butter until fruit is just tender. Add sugar, cinnamon, salt, and Bourbon. Fill crêpes, roll up, sprinkle with chopped nuts. Makes 12 to 16.

Quick Nesselrode Crêpes

1 package vanilla pudding (3   ¼ cup finely chopped
  ounces)   candied fruit
1½ cups prepared eggnog

Prepare Eggnog Crêpes (page 26). Make vanilla pudding as directed on the package, but substitute 1½ cup eggnog for the prescribed milk. Cool, stirring occasionally. Add chopped fruit. Reheat crêpes, if desired, or use them cooled. Fill crêpes, roll up. Fills 16 crêpes.

Crêpes Melba

12 peach halves, canned or   1 package (about 10 ounces)
  fresh   frozen raspberries, pureed
1 pint vanilla ice cream

Make Eggnog Crêpes (page 26), keep warm. Arrange a peach half on each crêpe, fill the hollow with ice cream. Fold the crêpes over, top with pureed raspberries. Fills 12 crêpes.

Mandarin Crêpes

Juice of ½ lemon   1 can (1 pound) mandarin
3 tablespoons sugar   oranges, drained
½ cup cherry brandy   ½ cup prepared eggnog

Make Eggnog Crêpes (page 26), turning once to brown both sides; keep warm. Combine lemon juice and sugar in a skillet, stir until sugar is golden. Add brandy, heat. Add mandarins, simmer until sauce is thick. Stir in eggnog. Fold the crêpes in quarters, arrange on serving plates, spoon hot fruit sauce over them. Makes enough for 16 to 20 crêpes.

17
Tortilla Crêpes

Try these Southwestern and Mexican-accented fillings with Tortilla Crêpes (page 26). The sharp seasonings are a perfect foil for the characteristic slightly sweet flavor of corn-meal masa in the crêpes, and the smooth textures are ideal with the slight chewiness of these crêpes. Fill and roll hot crêpes as usual, or spread zesty cold fillings on crêpes, roll up and eat.

Appetizer Crêpes

Guacamole
(Avocado Paste)

Mash ripe avocado with fork, season to taste with lime or lemon juice and salt, grated onion, chopped pimiento or tomato, ground coriander or fresh coriander leaves, chopped chilies, hot pepper sauce. Taste as you go. Spread on warm Tortilla Crêpes (page 26) and roll up, or make a stack of small crêpes and spread each with guacamole.

Tacos
(Fried Stuffed Tortillas)

The tacos may be stuffed before or after frying. Fill the Tortilla Crêpes (page 26), fold, or roll them to hold the filling, and fry in deep fat.

Suitable fillings for Tacos: Fill with any of the tortilla fillings in the next column, top with shredded lettuce, jack cheese, chopped raw onion, sliced avocado or Guacamole, Mexican chili sauce, to your taste.

Pequenos Perros
(Little Dogs)

1 pound (10) frankfurters	**Mexican-style chili sauce or hot green chili spread**

Make Tortilla Crêpes (page 26). Arrange a frankfurter on each tortilla, spread lightly with hot sauce. Roll up. Bake seam side down, in a moderate oven (350°F.) until franks are heated through. Cut each into four sections. Serve as appetizers. Makes 40.

Albondigas de Tortilla
(Tortilla Balls)

These are made with leftover Tortilla Crêpes, and are so good it's worth making extras for the purpose.

6 leftover Tortilla Crêpes (page 26)	**1 tablespoon butter**
¼ pound soft cheese such as Brie	**1 egg**
	Salt and pepper

Soak the crêpes in water, drain and blend with the cheese, melted butter, egg, and seasoning. This is quickest done in a blender. Make into small balls and fry until brown. Serve hot.

Sopa de Albondigas de Tortilla
(Tortilla Ball Soup)

Prepare Tortilla Balls as above. Heat clear chicken broth, add Tortilla Balls, and serve with additional grated cheese.

Main Dish Crêpes

Relleno de Carne Picante
(Beef Filling)

1 pound lean ground beef	**½ cup Mexican red chili sauce**
1 tablespoon oil	
1 onion, chopped	

Make Tortilla Crêpes (page 26), keep warm. Cook meat in oil, stirring with a fork until the meat loses its color. Add onion, cook until soft. Drain fat. Add red chili sauce, simmer 1 minute. Makes about 2 cups. Spoon onto Tortillas, roll up. Fills 8 to 10.

Pork or Chicken Filling

1 onion, chopped	**1 small hot chili, minced**
1 tablespoon oil	**¼ cup raisins**
2 cups diced cooked pork, chicken or turkey	**⅔ cup Mexican red chili sauce**

Make Tortilla Crêpes (page 26), keep warm. Cook onion in oil, add meat or poultry, chili, raisins, and chili sauce. Spoon onto Tortillas, roll up. Fills 12 to 16.

Cheese and Chilies

Make Tortilla Crêpes (page 26). On each Tortilla place a slice of green chili, free of seeds and pith, and a stick of jack cheese, 1 by 4 by ½ inch. Fold Tortilla over cheese, fasten with a wooden pick. Brown in shallow hot fat until crisp; or heat on an ungreased griddle to melt cheese.

Or, mix 1 can (7 ounces) green chilies, 1 pound jack cheese, both shredded, spoon on Tortillas, heat on a griddle to melt cheese. Fills 12 to 16.

Chorizo Sausage

Make Tortilla Crêpes (page 26), keep warm. Peel off and discard casing of 1 pound chorizos, crumble or chop meat and brown in skillet. Pour off excess fat. Use as is, or add browned ground beef and Mexican red chili sauce for extra spiciness. Spoon onto Tortillas, roll. Fills 12 to 16.

Tostadas Compuestas
(Stuffed Toasted Tortillas)

Make Tortilla Crêpes (page 26), fry until crisp in hot oil. Spread each tortilla with hot Refried Beans (page 89), sprinkle with cooked chorizo that has been removed from skin, or chicken, turkey or pork, or with ground Beef filling (above) and grated Monterey jack cheese. Put under broiler to melt cheese. Sprinkle with chopped lettuce, garnish with avocado slices.

YOU CAN—

BEAT

STIR

WHIP

TURN

MIX

BLEND
THE CRÊPE

Flaming Chocolate Sauce for Crêpes (*page 56*)

Bananas and Cream Crêpes

Preparing crêpe liners for Lobster Soufflé Crêpes

Crêpes Used to Line Casserole (*page 41*)

Cherries Jubilee Crêpes *(page 86)*

Chocolate Mousse Crêpes (*page 37*)

Roast Beef with Horseradish Sauce for Blini (*page 78*)

Ricotta Crêpes (*page 66*)

Cranberry Blintzes (page 69)

Crêpes Suzette *(page 117)*

Whipped Cottage Cheese with
Brandied Strawberries for Crêpes *(page 38)*

Variation: Substitute crab meat for the cooked meat and the cheese. Garnish with mashed avocados seasoned with lime juice and garlic salt, sliced tomatoes, and ripe olives. Do not broil.

Chimichangas
(Deep-Fried Stuffed Tortillas)

Make Tortilla Crêpes (page 26). Make Beef Filling (page 88), fill Tortillas. Fold, fasten with wooden picks. Fry in 1 inch hot oil, 1 to 2 minutes. Drain on paper towels. Garnish with shredded Cheddar cheese, shredded lettuce, chopped radishes or onion.

Frijoles Refritos
(Refried Beans)

1 pound dried pinto or pink beans	2 teaspoons salt
5 cups water	1 cup bacon drippings or lard
1 onion, minced	

Make Tortilla Crêpes (page 26). Combine beans and water, bring to a boil, let stand covered for 2 hours or overnight. Add additional water if necessary to cover generously. Add onion and salt. Bring to a boil, simmer until beans are very tender, about 2 hours. Mash with a potato masher. Place in heavy skillet with half the bacon drippings. Cook over very low heat, stirring occasionally and adding more fat as needed, until beans are thickened and fat is absorbed. The more fat is stirred in, the lighter and creamier the frijoles will be! Serve in your own style —in folded crêpes or heaped on tortillas or using fried tortilla quarters as scoopers.

18
Whole Wheat Crêpes

Fanciers of whole wheat bread will be enchanted with the rich, satisfying taste of Whole Wheat Crêpes (page 27). Extra egg yolks add extra richness and creaminess to crêpes, while natural grains add healthful roughage. An ideal crêpe for the adventurous gourmet and the nutritionally aware. Whole Wheat Crêpes add distinction to a variety of fillings in addition to those based on fresh fruit and yogurt—some savory, some sweet, all worthy additions to your crêpe repertoire.

Appetizer Crêpes

Nutted Cream Cheese Whip Crêpes

1 cup walnuts or pecans, coarsely chopped	1 cup softened cream cheese ½ cup raisins

Prepare Whole Wheat Crêpes (page 27). Combine nuts, cheese, and raisins and mix well. Spread onto crêpes and roll up. Fills about 16.

Easy Liver Pâté Crêpes

4 slices bacon	¼ cup cream cheese
1 small onion, finely minced	Nutmeg to taste
½ pound braunschweiger sausage	

Prepare Whole Wheat Crêpes (page 27). Cook bacon until lightly browned but not crisp. Remove and drain on absorbent paper. Cook onion in bacon drippings until translucent. Put bacon, onion, sausage, and cream cheese through the finest blade of a meat grinder or into food processor, to make a smooth paste. Season to taste. Refrigerate for 2 hours. Spread on crêpes and roll up. Fills about 10.

Mussels Ravigote Crêpes

2 cups cooked or canned mussels, drained	Salt and pepper to taste
1 cup mayonnaise	Juice of ½ lemon
2 tablespoons Dijon-style mustard	1 tablespoon drained capers
	1 teaspoon fines herbes

Prepare Whole Wheat Crêpes (page 27). Combine mussels with remaining ingredients, mix well. Spoon onto crêpes and roll up. Arrange seam side down on a serving platter, cover and refrigerate until serving time. Fills about 16.

Western Crêpes

1 green pepper, chopped	Salt and pepper to taste
1 medium onion, chopped	4 eggs, beaten
½ cup cooked ham, chopped	Grated Cheddar cheese
4 tablespoons butter	

Make Whole Wheat Crêpes (page 27). In a large, heavy-bottomed skillet, cook green pepper, onion, and ham in butter, stirring occasionally, until vegetables are wilted. Pour in eggs and cook, stirring constantly, until eggs are set but still moist. Spoon mixture onto crêpes and roll up. Arrange seam side down in a lightly buttered baking dish and sprinkle with grated cheese. Bake in a hot oven (425°F.) 10 minutes, or until cheese is melted and golden brown. Fills about 8.

Main Dish Crêpes

Fish in Green Sauce Crêpes

1 pound firm white-fleshed fish fillets	¼ cup dry white wine
Flour for dredging	2 cloves garlic, minced
4 tablespoons olive oil	¼ cup finely chopped parsley
¼ cup finely chopped onions	½ teaspoon salt
¾ cup water	¼ cup cooked green peas (optional)

Make Whole Wheat Crêpes (page 27). Dredge fillets in flour and dust off excess. Heat oil in a heavy-bottomed skillet and cook fillets until evenly colored on both sides, about 4 minutes. Remove to absorbent paper and cut into ½-inch pieces. Cook onions in remaining oil, stirring frequently, or until translucent. Stir in 1 tablespoon flour and cook, stirring constantly, for about 2 minutes. Stir in water and wine and cook over moderate heat, stirring until sauce thickens. Mash garlic, parsley, and salt to a smooth paste and stir the paste into the simmering sauce. Divide cooked fish and peas onto the crêpes and roll up. Arrange seam side down in a buttered, shallow baking dish, cover with the green sauce. Bake in a 425°F. oven until sauce is steaming hot, about 10 minutes. Fills about 8.

Turkey Marka

2 cups cooked, white-meat turkey cubes	½ cup black olives, drained, pitted, and cut in rounds
Salt and pepper to taste	½ cup sour cream
Juice of ½ lemon	Chopped parsley

Make Whole Wheat Crêpes (page 27). Season turkey cubes with salt, pepper, and lemon juice and allow to marinate for 30 minutes. Combine with olives and sour cream. Spoon onto crêpes, roll up, and refrigerate until serving time. Garnish with chopped parsley, serve with more sour cream. Fills about 12.

Lamb Curry Crêpes

1 green cooking apple, peeled, and coarsely chopped	½ teaspoon powdered ginger
	Salt and freshly ground black pepper to taste
1 small onion, chopped	1 teaspoon sugar
2 cloves garlic, minced	¼ cup coconut milk (optional)
6 tablespoons oil	
3 tablespoons curry powder	1 pound boned lamb, trimmed and cut in ¾-inch cubes
4 tablespoons flour	
1 tablespoon tomato paste	
Juice of 1 lemon	Oil for browning
2 cups chicken or beef broth	¼ cup heavy cream

Prepare Whole Wheat Crêpes (page 27). Cook apple, onion, and garlic in oil until vegetables are wilted. Sprinkle with curry powder and flour, and cook, stirring constantly, for 4 minutes (do not allow curry powder to burn or scorch). Stir in remaining ingredients, except the lamb, oil, and heavy cream. Quickly brown lamb cubes in hot oil and stir into simmering sauce. Cook uncovered, over moderate heat, for 1½ to 2 hours or until sauce is thickened and lamb is tender. Spoon meat and vegetables onto crêpes. Arrange, seam side down in a shallow baking dish. Strain the sauce, mix with cream, pour over the filled crêpes. Bake in a hot oven (375°F.) for 35 minutes. Makes 4 to 6 servings.

Cheese Crêpes Béchamel

1 cup chopped ham	1¾ cups chicken broth
1 cup grated Gruyère or	¼ cup cream
Swiss cheese (4 ounces)	Salt, pepper
BECHAMEL SAUCE:	TOPPING:
1 small onion, minced	¼ cup grated Parmesan
¼ cup butter	cheese
¼ cup flour	

Make Whole Wheat Crêpes (page 27). Divide ham and cheese onto crêpes, fold into quarters. Arrange in a buttered shallow baking dish. Cook onion in butter until golden, sprinkle with flour, cook, stirring, for a moment. Gradually stir in chicken broth and cook, stirring, until sauce is thickened and smooth. Add cream, season to taste with salt and pepper. Pour this Béchamel Sauce over the filled crêpes. Sprinkle with Parmesan. Bake in a hot oven (400°F.) until the cheese melts and the sauce is bubbling hot. Serves 8.

Crêpes Florentine

1 small onion, finely chopped	4 cups water
2 cloves garlic, minced	½ cup vinegar
4 tablespoons butter	8 eggs
1 pound fresh spinach,	1 cup Béchamel Sauce
cleaned and chopped	(above)
Salt and freshly ground	¼ cup Parmesan cheese,
pepper to taste	grated
Pinch nutmeg	

Prepare Whole Wheat Crêpes (page 27). Cook onions and garlic in butter until onions are translucent. Add spinach and continue cooking, stirring frequently, until spinach is wilted. Remove from heat and stir in salt, pepper, and nutmeg. Bring water and vinegar to a boil, reduce to simmering. Slip eggs into the water from a saucer, one at a time. Cook until whites are opaque and yolks still soft. Remove with a slotted spoon to a plate of cold water. Spoon spinach on the crêpes, top each with a poached egg, roll up. Arrange seam side down in a shallow baking dish, cover with Béchamel Sauce, and sprinkle with

Parmesan cheese. Bake in a 425°F. oven 15 minutes or until golden brown. Fills 8.

Dessert Crêpes

Yogurt, Honey, and Raisin Compote Crêpes

½ cup honey	Grated rind of 1 lemon
¼ cup water	1 cup plain yogurt
1½ cups raisins	Honey to garnish

Make Whole Wheat Crêpes (page 27). Combine honey, water, raisins, and grated lemon rind in a heavy-bottomed saucepan, bring to a boil, and cook, stirring frequently, until syrup is reduced by half. Spoon onto crêpes, roll up, and arrange seam side down on a serving platter. Top with yogurt and drizzle with honey to garnish. Fills about 8.

Tropical Crêpes

2 ripe bananas	2 tablespoons dark rum
1 cup sour cream	¼ cup dark brown sugar

Make Whole Wheat Crêpes (page 27). In a blender or food mill, mash bananas to a smooth paste. Combine with sour cream, rum, and brown sugar and mix until evenly blended. Spoon onto crêpes, roll up, and arrange seam side down on a serving platter. Refrigerate at least 2 hours. Moisten with a little more dark rum before serving, if desired. Fills 16.

Prune Whip Crêpes

1 cup pitted prunes	Cream of tartar
Water	1 tablespoon cocoa
Juice of 1 lemon	1 tablespoon confectioners'
½ cup sugar	sugar
3 egg whites	

Make Whole Wheat Crêpes (page 27). Simmer prunes in boiling water to cover for 10 minutes to plump. Drain the fruit, cool slightly, and puree in a blender or food mill. Combine puree, lemon juice, and ¼ cup sugar and mix well. Beat egg whites with a pinch of cream of tartar until they form soft peaks. Gradually beat in remaining sugar and beat until stiff. Mix ⅓ egg whites thoroughly with the prune mixture. Gently fold in remaining egg whites. Spoon onto crêpes, roll up, and arrange seam side down on a serving platter. Cover and refrigerate at least 2 hours before serving. Combine cocoa and confectioners' sugar and sift over crêpes just before serving. Fills about 12.

Frozen Cream Cheese Filling for Crêpes

**6 ounces cream cheese, cut
   in cubes
2 cups light cream**
**⅔ cup sugar
1 teaspoon vanilla
Confectioners' sugar**

Make Whole Wheat Crêpes (page 27). Whirl cheese, cream, sugar, and vanilla in a blender at high speed for 10 seconds until smooth. Pour into ice-cube tray, cover, and freeze until edges are firm. Remove and beat until light and smooth. Return it to the tray, cover with foil, and freeze until firm. To serve, remove from freezer, spoon onto crêpes, and roll up. Sprinkle with confectioners' sugar or serve with fruit or chocolate sauce. Fills about 12 crêpes.

Ricotta Strawberry Crêpes

**1 pint strawberries
1 pint ricotta cheese
1 tablespoon honey**
**½ teaspoon grated lemon
   rind**

Prepare Whole Wheat Crêpes (page 27). Hull and halve berries. Combine cheese with honey and lemon rind. Fold in berries. Spoon onto crêpes. Roll. Makes filling for about 16 crêpes.

19
Sourdough Crêpes

The same qualities that make sourdough bread a favorite with people who know and love bread are apparent in Sourdough Crêpes (page 27) . . . a natural toothsomeness and effervescence of texture and flavor, a brightness that lends distinction to a variety of fillings from pungent black olives and Italian ham to an exotic ice cream made with avocado and pistachio nuts.

Appetizer Crêpes

Blue Cheese Spread

¼ pound blue cheese
¼ cup olive oil
2 cloves garlic
2 tablespoons brandy or
  Cognac

Dash of Worcestershire
  sauce

Prepare Sourdough Crêpes (page 27). Blend blue cheese with olive oil. Mash garlic cloves with brandy and Worcestershire sauce. Combine with blue cheese mixture. Spread evenly over each crêpe and roll up. Serve at room temperature, or heat briefly under the broiler. Fills about 8 to 12 crêpes.

Black Olives and Sour Cream

1 clove garlic
½ teaspoon salt
½ teaspoon pepper
1 cup black olives, drained,
  pitted, and chopped

1 tablespoon prepared horseradish
1 cup sour cream

Prepare Sourdough Crêpes (page 27). Mash garlic with salt and pepper. Combine with chopped olives and horseradish. Gently fold in sour cream. Spoon mixture onto center of cool crêpes, roll up, and arrange seam side down on serving platter. Fills about 10 crêpes.

Fried Oyster Crêpes

24 large oysters
2 eggs
½ teaspoon salt
⅛ teaspoon pepper

2 tablespoons cold water
1 cup bread crumbs
Mayonnaise

Prepare 4 Sourdough Crêpes (page 27). Wash and drain oysters. Beat eggs with seasonings, add water, and mix. Dip oysters into the egg wash, then into the crumbs. Refrigerate for 5 minutes before frying. Fry in deep fat (375° to 380°F.) until brown, about 2 minutes. Cut crêpes in half, spread with mayonnaise, place 3 oysters close to cut side, roll. Makes 8 appetizer servings.

Main Dish Crêpes

Apple and Sausage Stuffed Crêpes

2 cooking apples, peeled,
  cored, and chopped
1 small onion, coarsely
  chopped
3 tablespoons butter

1 pound well-seasoned pork-
  sausage meat
2 tablespoons chopped
  parsley
1 cup tomato sauce

Prepare Sourdough Crêpes (page 27). Sauté apples and onions in butter until just tender but not mushy. Stir in pork sausage and continue cooking, stirring occasionally, until meat has lost its pink color. Remove from heat and stir in parsley. Spoon onto crêpes and roll up. Arrange, seam side down, in a shallow baking dish and top with tomato sauce. Bake in a moderately hot oven (375°F.) 35 minutes. Fills about 16 crêpes.

Western Sourdough Crêpes

1 tablespoon chopped ham
1 tablespoon chopped onion
1 tablespoon chopped green
  pepper

1 tablespoon butter
2 eggs
2 tablespoons milk
Salt, pepper

Make 2 Sourdough Crêpes (page 27), keep warm. Cook ham, onion, and green pepper in butter until onions are translucent. Beat eggs with milk, seasoning, add to pan, stir until mixture is set but still creamy. Divide mixture onto crêpes, roll up, serve hot. Makes 1 hearty serving.

Crêpes Carbonara

8 strips bacon, cut into ½-
  inch pieces
1 medium onion, finely
  minced
2 cloves garlic, minced
1 cup prosciutto or Italian
  ham, coarsely chopped
2 eggs, lightly beaten

1 cup fontina or Swiss
  cheese, grated
Salt and freshly ground
  black pepper to taste
½ cup Parmesan cheese,
  grated
¼ cup chopped parsley

Prepare Sourdough Crêpes (page 27). Cool, cut in thin strips to resemble cooked spaghetti. Sauté bacon in a heavy skillet until lightly browned and remove to absorbent paper to drain. Cook onions, garlic, and prosciutto in bacon drippings until onions are wilted. To assemble, separate crêpe strips in a warmed serving dish and top with the bacon pieces and the onion, garlic, and prosciutto mixture. Add the beaten eggs, fontina cheese, salt, pepper, Parmesan cheese, and parsley and toss well. Makes about 6 servings.

Sourdough Onion Tart

1½ cups sliced onions
¼ cup butter
1 tablespoon chopped fresh
  oregano or 1 teaspoon
  dried oregano
1 teaspoon salt

3 eggs, lightly beaten
1½ cups sour cream
Salt and freshly ground
  black pepper to taste
½ cup grated Swiss or
  Gruyère cheese

Prepare Sourdough Crêpes (page 27), allow to cool, and arrange in the bottom of a 9-inch pie plate, overlapping edges to form a bottom crust. Cook onions in butter until translucent. Season with oregano and salt. Spread onions over crêpes in bottom of pie plate. Mix eggs, sour cream, salt, and pepper, and pour over onions. Sprinkle with grated cheese and bake in a hot oven (400°F.) 15 minutes or until top is golden brown. Remove from oven and let stand 10 minutes before serving. Makes about 6 servings.

Creamed Salmon Crêpes

3 tablespoons butter	Salt and pepper to taste
3 tablespoons flour	½ cup cooked or canned
1 cup milk	salmon, flaked
¼ cup grated Swiss cheese	

Make Sourdough Crêpes (page 27). Melt butter, add flour, and cook for a moment, stirring. Gradually stir in milk and cook, stirring, until the sauce is thick and smooth. Add cheese, stir until cheese melts. Season to taste with salt and pepper and fold in salmon. Spoon mixture onto crêpes, roll, and serve. Fills about 8 crêpes.

Wild Mushrooms and Cream Crêpes

½ pound mushrooms, chanterelles or cultivated	Salt, pepper
3 tablespoons butter	1 cup heavy cream

Prepare Sourdough Crêpes (page 27) and keep warm. Pick chanterelles in season, or buy a pint basket of mushrooms. Trim stems, wipe mushrooms clean with a moist cloth. Slice large mushrooms lengthwise and leave small ones whole. Heat butter, season mushrooms, and add to pan. Cook until mushrooms brown lightly. Cover pan and cook five minutes more, until mushrooms release liquid. Add cream and cook gently, uncovered, until sauce thickens. Adjust seasonings, add a little paprika if desired. Spoon mushrooms onto warm crêpes, roll or fold up. Fills about 8 crêpes.

Duckling and Prune Compote Crêpes

2 cups water	⅛ teaspoon cayenne
2 cups prunes	2 tablespoons lemon juice
1 clove garlic, minced	2 tablespoons raspberry jam
2 tablespoons finely chopped coriander	2 cups cooked duckling meat, cut in uniform slices
¼ teaspoon salt	2 tablespoons butter

Prepare Sourdough Crêpes (page 27). Bring water to a boil, drop in prunes, turn down heat, and simmer until prunes are tender. Drain (reserve cooking liquid) and remove pits. Combine pitted prunes with remaining ingredients except the duckling and butter and puree in a blender, gradually adding cooking liquid until it is all incorporated. Divide duck meat among crêpes, moisten with prune sauce, and roll up. Arrange crêpes, seam side down, in a shallow baking dish. Cover with remaining sauce, dot with butter, and bake in a moderately hot oven (400°F.) until sauce is bubbling hot or about 15 minutes. Fills 16 crêpes.

Dessert Crêpes

Kir Crêpes

1 pint lemon sherbet	Grated rind of 1 lemon
4 ounces Crème de Cassis or blackberry brandy	¼ cup toasted hazelnuts, finely grated
Pinch of salt	Confectioners' sugar

Prepare Sourdough Crêpes (page 27). Remove sherbet from freezer and allow to soften 15 minutes at room temperature. Combine softened sherbet with the Cassis, salt, lemon rind, and ground hazelnuts, beat until smooth. Spoon onto crêpes, roll up. Arrange on a serving tray, seam side down, cover with foil, and store in freezer until serving time. Sprinkle with confectioners' sugar. Fills about 16 crêpes.

Boysenberry Crêpes

2 cups fresh boysenberries	1 cup heavy cream, sweetened and whipped stiff
¼ cup sugar	Confectioners' sugar
1 cup water	
2 tablespoons Crème de Cassis or kirsch	

Prepare Sourdough Crêpes (page 27). Clean berries. Bring sugar and water to a boil. Add berries, simmer until just tender but still hold their shape. Drain and cool (reserve poaching syrup for other use). Gently fold liqueur and chilled berries into whipped cream. Spoon onto crêpes and refrigerate at least 2 hours, or freeze 1 hour. Sprinkle with confectioners' sugar. Fills about 16.

Tip: To use canned berries, drain the berries and sprinkle them with ¼ cup sugar, let stand 30 minutes, and then fold into whipped cream.

Apple Crêpes

1 can (1 pound) pie-sliced apples	½ teaspoon salt
¼ cup butter, melted	½ teaspoon cinnamon
½ cup brown sugar	1 tablespoon brandy, rum, or liqueur

Make Sourdough Crêpes (page 27). Mix apples with butter, sugar, salt, and cinnamon, heat. Add brandy. Spoon apple mixture onto crêpes, roll up, and serve at once. Fills about 16 crêpes.

Avocado and Pistachio Ice Cream Crêpes

1 pint vanilla ice cream	4 tablespoons heavy cream
1 ripe avocado, peeled and seeded	¼ cup shelled pistachio nuts
	⅛ teaspoon almond extract
¼ cup sugar	Green food coloring

Prepare Sourdough Crêpes (page 27). Remove ice cream from freezer and let stand 15 minutes to soften. Meanwhile puree avocado, sugar, and heavy cream to a smooth paste in a blender or food mill. Blend avocado mixture into ice cream and stir in pistachio nuts and almond extract. Adjust coloring to approximate the green of the ripe avocado. Spoon onto crêpes and roll up. Arrange on serving platter, cover with foil, and set in freezer for at least 4 hours. Fills about 12.

Raisin Cider Crêpes

3 tablespoons brown sugar	Pinch nutmeg or mace
1 tablespoon cornstarch	1 cup apple cider
¼ teaspoon salt	½ cup seedless raisins
¼ teaspoon cloves	1 teaspoon lemon juice
⅛ teaspoon cinnamon	

Prepare Sourdough Crêpes (page 27). Keep warm. In a heavy-bottomed saucepan, mix brown sugar, cornstarch, salt, cloves, cinnamon, and nutmeg. Stir in cider, raisins, and lemon juice and cook over high heat, stirring occasionally, until the mixture is thick and clear. Fold crêpes in quarters, arrange on a heated serving platter, and top with hot raisin sauce. Makes sauce for about 16 crêpes.

Honey Nougat Crêpes

½ cup honey	⅔ cup toasted hazelnuts, or almonds, chopped
3 cups sugar	
⅔ cup boiling water	⅔ cups candied cherries, chopped
2 egg whites	

Prepare Sourdough Crêpes (page 27), and brown lightly on both sides. Line the bottom of a 9-inch baking pan with cooked crêpes, reserving an equal number for the top crust. Combine honey, sugar, and boiling water in a heavy-bottomed saucepan, bring to a boil, and cook, stirring constantly, until liquid reaches 230°F. on a candy thermometer and will spin a 2-inch thread when a little is dropped from a fork or spoon. Beat egg whites until stiff but not dry. Pour ⅔ cup of the syrup into the egg whites, beating constantly while pouring. Heat the remaining syrup to 265°F. on a candy thermometer—a little will form a hard ball in cold water—and pour into egg-white mixture, beating as you pour. Continue beating until the candy begins to thicken. Add nuts and cherries, and pour into prepared pan. Top with remaining crêpes. Cut into 1-inch squares. Makes about 48 pieces.

20
Bran Crêpes

The crunchy texture and nutty flavor of crêpes made with whole bran have special appeal, to say nothing of the fiber values. These same attributes make Bran Crêpes (page 27) a gourmet's choice for fillings as diverse as shrimp pâté and liqueur-flavored cream cheese. Any one of these fillings would be most complementary to other sweetened crêpes, but the subtle, earthy taste of bran has a unique charm all its own.

Appetizer Crêpes

Chutney Cream Cheese Crêpes

½ cup chutney (preferably
    Major Grey's)
½ pound cream cheese

¼ teaspoon turmeric
¼ teaspoon grated ginger
    root

Make Bran Crêpes (page 27). Cream together chutney, cream cheese, turmeric, and ginger root. Spread mixture evenly on crêpes, roll up. Chill at least 2 hours to firm cheese before serving. Fills about 12.

Southern Shrimp Pâté Crêpes

1½ pounds shrimp, cooked,
    shelled, and deveined
½ cup butter, softened
Salt to taste
½ teaspoon freshly ground
    black pepper

1 tablespoon Worcestershire
    sauce
¼ teasoon hot pepper sauce
½ teaspoon nutmeg

Make Bran Crêpes (page 27). Put shrimp through the fine blade of a meat grinder. Blend with butter. Gradually beat in seasonings. Divide onto crêpes and roll up. Arrange crêpes side by side in a buttered, shallow baking dish and bake in a hot oven (425°F.) for 10 to 12 minutes. Fills about 16.

Puree of Garlic and Garbanzos for Bran Crêpes

2 cups cooked, canned gar-
    banzos (chick peas),
    drained and rinsed
1 cup water
1 teaspoon salt
6 cloves garlic, finely minced

¼ cup lemon juice
½ cup finely ground sesame
    seeds or almonds
1 medium onion, finely
    minced

Make Bran Crêpes (page 27). Simmer garbanzos in water with salt for about 1 hour, until very tender. Drain cooking liquid and reserve. In a blender, whirl the garbanzos with garlic and remaining ingredients, adding up to ¾ cup cooking liquid as necessary to make a fluffy mixture that will hold its shape. Spoon onto crêpes, roll up. Chill at least 3 hours before serving. Fills about 24.

Taramasalata Crêpes

6 slices white bread, crusts
    removed
1 cup cold water
4 ounces tarama (salted carp
    roe)

¼ cup lemon juice
¼ cup onion, finely grated
⅛ teaspoon freshly ground
    white pepper
¾ cup olive oil

Make Bran Crêpes (page 27). Soak bread in cold water for 5 minutes, squeeze dry, and mash with the back of a spoon. Beat in the tarama, one teaspoon at a time. Add lemon juice, onions, and pepper and continue beating to make a smooth paste. Grad-

ually beat in the oil, drop by drop at first and then in a thin stream until mixture is thick as mayonnaise. Spoon mixture onto crêpes and roll up. Refrigerate until serving time. Fills about 16.

Main Dish Crêpes

Turkish Lamb Crêpes

1 pound ground lamb
1 onion, chopped
¼ teaspoon oregano
½ teaspoon salt

Pepper
1 tablespoon flour
¼ cup water or bouillon
¼ cup pine nuts

Make Bran Crêpes (page 27) and keep warm. Cook lamb in a skillet, stirring with a fork until it is no longer pink. Pour off and discard excess fat. Add onion, oregano, and salt and pepper to taste; cook until onion is translucent. Sprinkle with flour, stir, add water, simmer for a minute to thicken. Add pine nuts and adjust seasoning. Spoon generously onto prepared crêpes. Roll. Makes 8 crêpes.

Crêpes Dolmeh

6 tablespoons oil
½ cup finely chopped onions
½ pound lean ground lamb
1½ cups cooked rice
½ cup currants or sultana
    raisins
½ cup finely chopped
    parsley
¼ cup finely chopped fresh
    dill (or 2 tablespoons
    dried dill)

Juice of 1 lemon
½ teaspoon each of tur-
    meric, oregano, and
    cinnamon
1 teaspoon salt
6 tablespoons butter

Make Bran Crêpes (page 27). Heat oil in a heavy-bottomed skillet and sauté onions, stirring frequently, until golden brown. Stir in ground meat and cook until all traces of pink disappear. Drain excess oil from skillet and stir in the rice, currants, parsley, dill, lemon juice, turmeric, oregano, cinnamon, and salt. Cook, stirring occasionally for 4 to 5 minutes. Spoon mixture onto crêpes and roll up. Arrange seam side down, in a buttered shallow baking dish. Dot with butter and bake in a moderate oven (325°F.) for 25 minutes. Fills about 16.

Combo Crêpes

Thinly sliced tongue or ham
Thinly sliced cheese, easy-
    melting variety

1 can (4 ounces) mushrooms,
    drained

Cook Bran Crêpes (page 27) on one side only, turn out on a towel browned side up. Cover with a slice of meat, a slice of cheese, and a few mushroom slices. Fold up bottom one-fourth of the crêpe, fold in the sides, fold over to make a tight package. Brown quickly on both sides in hot bacon fat or butter, folded side down first. Serve hot.

Dessert Crêpes

Apple Roësti Crêpes

4 tablespoons honey
3 tart apples, peeled and
  cored
3 tablespoons butter
Juice of 1 lemon
Pinch each of salt, cinnamon, and mace

½ cup brown sugar or
  maple syrup
2 eggs, beaten
1 cup light cream

Substitute 4 tablespoons honey for 4 tablespoons milk in the basic Bran Crêpe batter (page 27), and make crêpes. Arrange crêpes overlapping in a shallow baking dish. Cook apples in butter until just tender, about 5 minutes. Add lemon juice, salt, cinnamon, mace, and brown sugar. Beat eggs with cream, toss with apple mixture. Pour into baking dish and bake in a moderately hot oven (375°F.) about 20 minutes. Makes about 6 servings.

Baltimore Crêpes
(Raisin-Filled Crêpes)

1½ cups raisins
1½ cups water
3 tablespoons flour
⅛ teaspoon salt
¾ cup brown sugar
2 egg yolks

Juice of 1 lemon
Grated rind of 1 lemon
½ teaspoon each of cinna-
  mon, mace, and ginger
2 tablespoons butter

Make Bran Crêpes (page 27). Meanwhile simmer raisins in water until plumped (about 6 minutes). Mix the flour, salt, sugar, and egg yolks, and slowly stir in some of the hot raisin liquid. Combine with remaining raisin mixture and cook until thickened. Do not boil. Remove from heat. Stir in lemon juice, lemon rind, spices, and butter. Cool to room temperature. Spoon onto crêpes and roll up. Arrange, seam side down, in a buttered shallow baking dish and bake in a moderate oven (350°F.) for 25 minutes or until golden brown and puffed. Serve warm with ice cream or Cheddar cheese. Makes about 12.

Ginger Pecan Pithiviers

½ cup toasted pecans
2 eggs
½ cup sugar
¼ cup softened butter
4 tablespoons flour
1 teaspoon grated, fresh
  ginger root or ½ teaspoon
  powdered ginger

Grated rind of 1 lemon
¼ cup Bourbon
Butter
Sugar

Make Bran Crêpes (page 27). Pound pecans in a mortar or grind them in a blender, adding one egg to form a paste. Remove paste to a bowl and add sugar, butter, flour, ginger, lemon rind, remaining egg, and Bourbon. Mix well. Spoon mixture onto crêpes. Roll up and arrange seam side down in a buttered shallow baking dish. Dot crêpes with butter and sprinkle with sugar. Bake in a moderately hot oven (350°F.) 25 minutes or until puffed and lightly browned. Serve warm with ice cream or whipped cream. Fills about 8.

21

Soy Flour Crêpes

Soy flour, high in protein and low in fat, makes crêpes that are the particular joy of vegetarians of all persuasions. Fill Soy Flour Crêpes (page 27) with nuts and seeds—from peanuts to sesame, alfalfa sprouts to avocados, and cabbage to carrots . . . there is no end to the vegetables you can use to fill these high-protein crêpes to make appetizing and satisfying meals.

Appetizer Crêpes

Seeded Peanut Butter Salad

¾ cup peanut butter   Shredded lettuce
¼ cup sunflower seeds   4 radishes, chopped

Prepare Soy Flour Crêpes (page 27), keep warm.
Whirl peanut butter and sunflower seeds in a blender
until seeds are still visible but dispersed in the peanut
butter. Spread mixture in center of crêpe, garnish
with lettuce and radish. Roll up crêpes cigar fashion,
secure with pick. Fills about 16 crêpes.

Sesame Spread Crêpes

½ cup sesame seeds   ¼ cup chopped pitted dates
1 cup cottage cheese
¼ cup chopped dried apri-
   cots

Prepare Soy Flour Crêpes (page 27), keep warm.
Whirl sesame seeds in a blender to a fine powder.
Add to cottage cheese. Combine with apricots and
dates. Spoon mixture into crêpes and roll up envelope style. Fills about 16 crêpes.

Carrot and Raisin Crêpes

1 cup grated carrots   ½ teaspoon nutmeg
1 cup raisins   ½ cup mayonnaise
½ teaspoon salt

Prepare Soy Flour Crêpes (page 27), cool. Combine
above ingredients and refrigerate for 30 minutes for
flavors to mellow. Spoon onto crêpes and roll up,
cigar fashion. Makes 16 crêpes.

Alfalfa Sprouts and Avocado Crêpes

1 cup alfalfa sprouts   ½ cup sour cream
1 avocado

To sprout alfalfa seeds: Place several layers of moist-
ened paper toweling on a tray. Spread alfalfa seeds
on toweling and keep moist by sprinkling with cold
water daily. Leave tray in a dark place. After 3 days,
the sprouts will be ready. One-fourth cup alfalfa seeds
yields 6 cups sprouts.

Make Soy Flour Crêpes (page 27), cool. Slice avocado in half and remove pit. Mash avocado meat
with fork, add sour cream to make a creamy consistency. Spoon mixture onto cold crêpes, top with
alfalfa sprouts. Roll up. Fills 16 crêpes.

Cashew Banana Salad Crêpes

6 medium bananas   ⅔ cup cashew nuts, chopped
⅓ cup mayonnaise   Lettuce
1½ tablespoons milk

Prepare Soy Flour Crêpes (page 27). Peel bananas,
cut in pieces. Beat mayonnaise with milk until
smooth, coat banana pieces with mayonnaise mixture. Roll in chopped cashews. Sprinkle shredded
lettuce along the center of each crêpe, place banana
on top of lettuce, fold flaps over. Makes 12 crêpes.

Main Dish Crêpes

Peanut Slaw Crêpes

2 cups shredded cabbage   ¼ cup sour cream
½ teaspoon salt   1 tablespoon sugar
¼ teaspoon onion powder   ¼ cup chopped salted pea-
1 tablespoon lemon juice   nuts

Make Soy Flour Crêpes (page 27), cool. Combine
cabbage with remaining ingredients. Refrigerate for
30 minutes. Spoon onto cool crêpes, roll up. Fills 12
crêpes.

Rice Creole Crêpes

3 cups tomato juice   Bay leaf
½ teaspoon salt   1 cup (6 ounces) brown rice
4 peppercorns   1 package (10 ounces) frozen
3 whole cloves   chopped okra, cooked

Make Soy Flour Crêpes (page 27), keep warm. Bring
tomato juice to boil in a heavy large pot. Stir in salt,
peppercorns, cloves, bay leaf, and rice. Bring to boil
again, lower heat, and cover. Simmer for about 1
hour. Add cooked okra, cook 15 minutes more, until
rice is tender but still slightly chewy. Remove bay
leaf. Spoon onto warm crêpes, roll up. Fills about
16 crêpes.

Broccoli Mornay Crêpes

1 pound fresh broccoli   ½ cup milk
Water   ½ cup grated Swiss cheese
1 tablespoon margarine   Dash Worcestershire sauce
1 tablespoon flour   Salt, pepper

Prepare Soy Flour Crêpes (page 27). Wash broccoli, slash stalks and steam in covered pot until
stalks are tender, about 10 to 15 minutes. Place
stalks and flowerets in crêpes, roll up. Arrange in buttered shallow baking pan. Prepare sauce; melt
margarine, stir in flour. Slowly add milk and cook,
stirring, until sauce is smooth and thickened. Add
cheese, Worcestershire sauce, and salt and pepper to
taste. Cook until cheese melts. Pour sauce over

crêpes. Bake in a hot oven (425°F.) for 15 minutes. Makes 16 crêpes.

Tomato and Egg Crêpes

3 tablespoons butter or margarine	6 eggs
1 medium onion, chopped	¼ cup milk
2 tomatoes, chopped	Salt, pepper
	¼ teaspoon basil

Prepare Soy Flour Crêpes (page 27), keep warm. Melt margarine in skillet, cook onion until translucent. Stir in tomatoes, lower heat. Beat eggs lightly, add milk and seasonings. Add to the skillet and cook over low heat, stirring, until thick. Spoon onto crêpes, roll up envelope style. Fills 8 crêpes.

Nutted Cream Cheese and Raisin Crêpes

8 ounces cream cheese	½ cup chopped walnuts
1 tablespoon lemon juice	Salt
½ cup raisins	

Prepare Soy Flour Crêpes (page 27), keep warm. Combine cream cheese with lemon and blend until of spreading consistency. Stir in remaining ingredients. Spread on crêpes, fold into quarters, serve. Fills 8 crêpes.

Eggplant and Cheese Crêpes

1 eggplant (about 1 pound)	Juice of lemon
1 onion, chopped	Salt
1 tomato, skinned and chopped	½ cup mozzarella cheese
⅓ cup olive oil	½ cup grated Parmesan cheese

Make Soy Flour Crêpes (page 27), keep warm. Bake eggplant in a hot oven (400°F.) for 25 minutes. Cool, remove skin, chop. Combine eggplant and remaining vegetables with oil, lemon juice, and salt to taste. Spoon mixture onto crêpes, roll up. Arrange seam side down, in buttered shallow flameproof dish. Sprinkle cheeses over crêpes. Cook under broiler for about 5 minutes, until cheese is is melted and lightly browned. Makes about 16 crêpes.

Zucchini and Red Peppers with Yogurt Hollandaise Crêpes

¼ cup vegetable oil	**YOGURT HOLLANDAISE:**
2 onions, sliced	2 egg yolks
3 zucchini, chopped (about 1 pound)	¾ cup yogurt
2 red peppers, seeded and sliced	½ tablespoon lemon juice
Salt, pepper to taste	Salt, paprika
2 teaspoons each oregano and sweet basil	

Prepare Soy Flour Crêpes (page 27), keep warm. Heat oil in a large skillet. Add onions, zucchini, red peppers, and seasonings. Cook until tender, stirring occasionally, about 5 minutes. *Prepare Yogurt Hollandaise:* Beat egg yolks, add yogurt and lemon juice. Stir in top of a double boiler, over hot water, until thick and smooth. Add seasonings to taste. Spoon vegetable mixture onto warm crêpes, roll up. Pour Yogurt Hollandaise Sauce over crêpes. Makes 16 crêpes.

Dessert Crêpes

Sunflower Honey Peanut Spread Crêpes

2 tablespoons sunflower seeds	2 tablespoons honey
1 cup peanut butter	

Make Soy Flour Crêpes (page 27), keep warm. Crush sunflower seeds with a mortar and pestle (or with the back of a wooden spoon). Mix with peanut butter and honey. Spread on crêpes, fold into quarters. Makes 16 crêpes.

Currant and Fresh Apple Crêpes

3 tablespoons butter	½ cup currants
2 tablespoons brown sugar	3 medium apples, sliced

Make Soy Flour Crêpes (page 27), keep warm. Melt butter in a saucepan. Stir in sugar. Add currants and apple slices and cook, stirring and turning the apples until the slices are glazed, about 4 to 5 minutes. Fold warm crêpes in quarters and fill pockets with mixture, using a slotted spoon. Pour sauce remaining in pan over crêpes. Fills about 16 crêpes.

Cheese Crêpes with Maple Yogurt Sauce

¾ cup cottage cheese	¾ cup yogurt
¼ cup chopped pitted prunes	¼ cup maple syrup

Prepare Soy Flour Crêpes (page 27), keep cold. Drain cottage cheese, blend with prunes. Fold crêpes into quarters and fill with cheese mixture. Blend yogurt and maple syrup, pour over crêpes just before serving. Makes 16 crêpes.

Honey Orange Crêpes

1 cup orange marmalade	Juice of lemon
½ cup honey	Grated rind of 1 lemon

Prepare Soy Flour Crêpes (page 27), fold into quarters, keep warm. Combine marmalade with honey and lemon juice and rind. Pour over crêpes. Makes sauce for 16 crêpes.

22

Buttermilk or Yogurt Crêpes

Use these lacy, fine-textured, and slightly tart Buttermilk or Yogurt Crêpes (page 27) to turn out extra-flavorful crêpes. Some of these have fillings for hearty appetites, and some have fillings for those who particularly enjoy natural foods.

Appetizer Crêpes

Blue Cheese and Apple Crêpes

4 tart apples
1 tablespoon butter
1 tablespoon brown sugar
Water as needed

1 cup diced ham
2 ounces blue cheese (½ cup crumbled)
Prepared mustard

Make Buttermilk or Yogurt Crêpes (page 27). Peel apples, quarter, slice thinly. Melt butter in skillet, add apples, cover, cook 3 minutes. Turn, sprinkle with brown sugar, add a little water to prevent sticking as necessary, cover and cook until fruit is barely tender, about 5 minutes in all. Reserve ¾ cup apple mixture for topping. Mix the remainder with the ham and cheese. Spoon mixture generously onto crêpes, roll up, arrange side by side in a shallow buttered baking dish. Season topping mixture to taste with mustard, spread on crêpes. Bake in a moderate oven (350°F.) about 10 minutes. Makes about 16 crêpes.

Clams and Corn Crêpes

½ cup cooked corn, pureed
½ cup cooked clams, chopped
½ teaspoon parsley, finely chopped
½ cup yogurt

2 hard-cooked eggs, finely chopped
¼ teaspoon prepared mustard
Butter

Prepare Buttermilk or Yogurt Crêpes (page 27). Mix together the corn, clams, parsley, 1 tablespoon of yogurt, eggs, and mustard. Spread onto crêpes and roll up. Arrange seam side down in a buttered baking dish. Cover with remaining yogurt and bake in a moderate oven (375°F.) 10 minutes or until filling is hot. Makes 4 servings.

Main Dish Crêpes

Rarebit Crêpes

2 tablespoons butter
1 pound sharp Cheddar cheese, grated
2 eggs, beaten
½ teaspoon salt

⅛ teaspoon cayenne
½ teaspoon dry mustard
Dash Worcestershire sauce
1 can of beer (12 ounces)
Paprika

Prepare Buttermilk or Yogurt Crêpes (page 27), keep warm. Melt butter in a double boiler over simmering water and stir in cheese. Cook, stirring, until cheese begins to melt. Meanwhile, combine eggs with seasonings and beer. Gradually stir into melted cheese. Cook, stirring constantly, until thickened. Serve at once over folded crêpes, sprinkle with paprika if desired. Makes 4 to 6 servings.

Blue Cheese and Chicken Crêpes

2 tablespoons butter
3 tablespoons flour
1½ cups milk
¼ pound blue cheese, crumbled (1 cup)

2 cups diced cooked chicken or turkey

Make Buttermilk or Yogurt Crêpes (page 27). Melt butter, stir in flour and cook for a minute, stirring. Gradually add milk and heat, stirring, until the sauce is smooth and thickened. Add cheese, stir until melted. Add half the sauce to the diced chicken, spoon generously onto prepared crêpes. Roll, arrange in a shallow buttered baking dish, seam side down. Pour remaining sauce over crêpes. Bake in a moderate oven (350°F.) about 10 minutes, until the sauce is bubbling hot. Makes about 20 crêpes.

Fruited Granola Crêpes

2 large Valencia oranges
3 ripe bananas

2 tablespoons honey
½ cup granola

Make Buttermilk or Yogurt Crêpes (page 27). Peel oranges, carefully removing all membranes, and cut into thin slices. Peel and cut bananas into thin slices. Combine oranges, bananas, and honey, and mix well. Add granola and toss to combine. Spoon onto crêpes, roll up, and arrange seam side down on a serving dish. Fills 8 crêpes.

Strawberries and Yogurt Crêpes

1 cup fresh strawberries, washed, hulled, and quartered
¼ cup sugar

¼ cup kirsch
Juice of ½ lemon
1 cup vanilla yogurt

Prepare Buttermilk or Yogurt Crêpes (page 27). Combine strawberries with sugar, kirsch, and lemon juice and let stand for 30 minutes. Drain strawberries and reserve liquid. Mix yogurt with fruit and spoon onto crêpes. Roll up, arrange seam side down on a serving dish, and drizzle with reserved liquid. Refrigerate until ready to serve. Fills about 8 crêpes.

Coffee Cream Crêpes

1 cup softened cream cheese
¼ cup sugar
4 teaspoons finely ground coffee

¼ cup rum

Prepare Buttermilk or Yogurt Crêpes (page 27). Put the cheese through a sieve, add sugar, coffee, and rum, and stir until smooth and thick. Spread the flavored cheese on the crêpes, roll up, and arrange seam side down on a serving platter. Refrigerate for 2 hours before serving so that the coffee flavor has time to develop. Fills about 16 crêpes.

Ricotta and Diced Fruit Crêpes

1 cup ricotta
2 egg yolks
¼ cup sugar
1 tablespoon brandy, rum,
  or kirsch

½ cup diced dried or
  candied fruit
Confectioners' sugar

Prepare Buttermilk or Yogurt Crêpes (page 27). Put ricotta into a sieve to drain. Beat the egg yolks and sugar. Beat in brandy and diced fruits. Add this mixture gradually to the sieved ricotta to make a thick cream. Spoon the cheese onto crêpes, roll up, and arrange seam side down on a serving dish. Refrigerate until ready to serve, sprinkle with confectioners' sugar. Fills about 16 crêpes.

Peach Crêpes

1 can (about 1 pound) sliced
  peaches in syrup
¼ cup honey or molasses

¼ cup yogurt
½ cup heavy cream, whipped

Make Buttermilk or Yogurt Crêpes (page 27). Drain syrup from fruit and reserve it for another use. Mix peaches with honey or molasses, yogurt, and whipped cream. Fill hot or cold crêpes, arrange folded side down on serving plates, top with remaining peach mixture. Makes about 16 crêpes.

Crêpes Georgette

Make batter for Buttermilk or Yogurt Crêpes (page 27). Use thin-sliced pineapple, fresh or canned fruit, well-drained. Pour the crêpe batter into the pan, add a little fruit and a little more batter to cover the fruit. Turn to brown both sides.

Variations: Instead of pineapple use banana, poached apple slices, canned apricots.

23
Low-Cholesterol Crêpes

These crêpes (page 27), made with low-fat rice flour, are designed for people who enjoy good food, but on the advice of a doctor must restrict their intake of saturated fats and calories. The fillings suggested also follow the principles of the low cholesterol diet regime. . . . No egg yolks are used, few whites of eggs, no red meat, and no foods high in saturated fats. It goes without saying that the same low-calorie, low-fat fillings may be used to fill the more conventional crêpes at your own discretion.

Appetizer Crêpes

Buttermilk, Cottage Cheese, and Radish Crêpes

1¾ cups drained low-fat cottage cheese	3 radishes, chopped
¼ cup buttermilk	Dash of celery salt

Make Low-Cholesterol Crêpes (page 27). Blend cottage cheese, buttermilk, and radishes. Season with spices to taste. Spoon mixture onto warm or cooled crêpes, roll. Makes 16 crêpes.

Cucumber in Dill Dressing Crêpes

3 small cucumbers	3 tablespoons water
3 tablespoons salt	1 tablespoon chopped fresh dill or 1 teaspoon dried dill
¾ cup vinegar	
3 tablespoons sugar	

Make Low-Cholesterol Crêpes (page 27). Score cucumbers with the tines of a fork and slice thin. Sprinkle with salt and set in refrigerator overnight. Drain, rinse in cold water, drain again. Combine remaining ingredients to make dressing, pour over cucumbers. Chill 2 hours before serving. Spoon cucumbers into crêpes with a slotted spoon. Roll up, cut in half, secure with picks. Serve sauce as dip. Makes about 16 crêpes.

Sardines in Wine Sauce Crêpes

1 can (1 pound) sardines in tomato sauce

Prepare Low-Cholesterol Crêpes (page 27). Cut in half. Drain sardines and bone; place one piece of sardine and some of sauce on each crêpe half and roll up into a cone. Secure with a toothpick. Makes 32 appetizer servings.

Cauliflower and Corn Relish Crêpes

1 small cauliflower, broken into flowerets	1 dill pickle, diced
1 can (12 ounces) whole kernel corn	3 tablespoons pickle juice
	1 tablespoon sugar

Make Low-Cholesterol Crêpes (page 27). Combine vegetables, pickle juice, and sugar in a bowl and marinate overnight. Spoon mixture into warm or cooled crêpes, roll. Makes 16 crêpes.

Main Dish Crêpes

Lemon-Seasoned Chicken Crêpes

2 tablespoons margarine	3 tablespoons chopped fresh parsley
2 chicken breasts, boned, skinned, and diced (2 cups)	Salt, pepper
Juice of 2 lemons	

Make Low-Cholesterol Crêpes (page 27). Melt margarine in skillet. Cook chicken for 5 minutes over moderate heat, stirring occasionally. Add lemon juice, chopped parsley, and seasonings to taste. Cover, simmer until chicken is tender. Spoon into crêpes, roll. Makes 8 crêpes.

Veal Piccata Crêpes

1 pound thin veal scallops	3 tablespoons vegetable oil
¼ cup flour	3 tablespoons lemon juice
1½ teaspoons salt	2 tablespoons minced parsley
¼ teaspoon white pepper	Lemon slices

Prepare Low-Cholesterol Crêpes (page 27), keep warm. Cut veal into 12 pieces, place the pieces between sheets of waxed paper, pound until thin. Dredge veal with flour seasoned with salt and pepper. Heat the oil in a skillet; cook veal until browned on both sides. Remove veal and keep warm. Stir lemon juice and parsley into the skillet juices, cook 30 seconds, scraping the pan to incorporate any browned particles. Place veal in crêpes and roll up envelope style. Pour the lemon sauce evenly over the crêpes. Garnish with lemon slices. Makes 12 crêpes.

Sole and Spinach Crêpes

1½ pounds fillet of sole	1 stalk celery
2 cups water	2 tablespoons corn oil or margarine
1½ teaspoons salt	
¼ teaspoon freshly ground black pepper	2 tablespoons flour
1 onion, sliced	1 cup cooked chopped seasoned spinach
1 bay leaf	

Prepare Low-Cholesterol Crêpes (page 27). Cut the fillets into 16 portions. Combine the water, salt, pepper, onion, bay leaf, and celery. Bring to a boil and cook over medium heat 10 minutes. Arrange the fish in the broth; cover the pan, simmer 5 minutes, or until fish flakes easily with a fork. Remove fish with a slotted spoon. Boil broth rapidly to reduce to 1 cup. Strain the broth. Melt oil in a saucepan; stir in flour, cook for a moment. Add broth, bring to a boil. Slowly, stirring constantly, cook for 5 minutes. Put half a fillet on each crêpe, top with spinach, fold. Arrange in a buttered shallow baking dish, cover with sauce. Bake in a moderate oven (350°F.) 10 to 15 minutes. Makes 16 hearty crêpes.

Walnut Carrot Spread Crêpes

8 medium carrots	2 tablespoons warm skim
½ cup water	milk
¾ cup chopped walnuts	½ teaspoon salt
	Dash of pepper

Prepare Low-Cholesterol Crêpes (page 27), keep warm. Wash and scrape carrots, slice thin. Cook in water until tender, about 10 minutes, drain and mash. Add walnuts and enough warm milk to moisten to spreading consistency. Season with salt and pepper to taste. Spoon mixture onto crêpes and roll up. Fills 16 crêpes.

Whiting Bouquetière Crêpes

1½ pounds whiting fillets	Pinch of ground thyme
1½ cups skim milk	10 peppercorns
1 bay leaf	1 slice of onion

Prepare Low-Cholesterol Crêpes (page 27), keep warm. Soak fish in milk for 1 hour in a skillet with bay leaf, thyme, peppercorns, and onion. Put skillet over heat, bring liquid to a boil, reduce heat, and simmer gently for 10 minutes until fish is cooked and will flake readily. Place serving of fish on lower edge of crêpe, roll up. Fills 12 crêpes.

Dessert Crêpes

Crêpes Meringue

1 can (about 1 pound) pine-apple chunks, drained	¼ teaspoon cream of tartar
	¼ cup sugar
3 egg whites	1 teaspoon vanilla extract
Dash salt	

Prepare Low-Cholesterol Crêpes (page 27). Fill with drained pineapple, roll up. Arrange seam side down on buttered shallow baking dish. Beat egg whites, salt, and cream of tartar until soft peaks begin to form. Gradually beat in the sugar, continue to beat until meringue is very thick. Add vanilla extract. Mound meringue on crêpes by tablespoons. Bake in a slow oven (300°F.) about 15 minutes, until meringue is golden. Makes about 16 crêpes.

Crêpes with Marmalade Soufflé

4 egg whites	3 tablespoons orange
1 tablespoon lemon juice	marmalade
2 tablespoons sugar	

Prepare Low-Cholesterol Crêpes (page 27), fold into quarters, and line greased custard cups, open end up. Beat egg whites until foamy, beat in lemon juice and sugar, 1 tablespoon at a time, and continue to beat until stiff. Fold in marmalade. Fill crêpe-lined cups. Place cups in a shallow dish in 2 inches of water. Bake in a moderate oven (300°F.) until the filling is firm. Makes about 6 to 8 crêpes.

Minted Crêpes

¼ cup Crème de Menthe	8 grapefruit sections
1 cup dry white wine	8 small clusters seedless
Juice of 2 lemons	grapes
Dash lime juice	2 bananas cut in chunks
4 pears, quartered	

Prepare Low-Cholesterol Crêpes (page 27), keep warm. Blend liqueur, wine, and juices in a bowl. Add pears, grapefruit, and grapes. Chill 1 hour, stirring occasionally. Fold crêpes into quarters. Fill pocket with marinated fruits and banana chunks. Pour liqueur marinade over crêpes. Fills about 12.

Brandied Crêpes Flambé

2 tablespoons cornstarch	1 cup water
¼ cup sugar	Brown food coloring
⅛ teaspoon salt	¼ cup brandy

Prepare Low-Cholesterol Crêpes (page 27), fold into quarters, keep warm on a chafing dish. Mix cornstarch, sugar, and salt together in a saucepan. Blend in water and food coloring. Cook over low heat, stirring constantly, until sauce is thick and clear. Heat brandy in a ladle, ignite it, and pour flaming over the crêpes. Makes 12 crêpes.

Tip: To make brown coloring mix together 4 drops red food coloring, 3 drops of yellow, and 1 drop of green.

Dried Fruit Crêpes

¾ pound snipped prunes or other dried fruit	2 tablespoons butter
	Lemon juice to taste
¼ cup candied fruit peel, chopped	2 tablespoons melted butter
	Confectioners' sugar
¼ cup rum or liqueur	
1 cup fruit syrup drained from canned peaches or pears	

Make Low-Cholesterol Crêpes (page 27). Cover prunes and peel with rum, let stand 2 hours, stirring occasionally. Add fruit syrup, cook until thick. Add butter and a dash of lemon juice to taste. Fill crêpes with mixture, roll. Arrange on flameproof serving dish. Brush crêpes with melted butter, dust with sugar. Glaze briefly under the broiler flame. Makes 16 crêpes.

Variation: Stack crêpes with fruit filling between layers, serve with ring of chocolate sauce.

24
Crêpes for a Crowd

When you're expecting a crowd, it's smart hospitality to put crêpes on the menu. Prepare the practical, easy-to-freeze Crêpes for a Crowd (page 27) in advance. When your guests are due to arrive, defrost the crêpes and fill them according to your special taste preferences. Crêpes can make trays of appetizers, or a company-worthy yet economical main dish, or desserts that may be prepared well in advance and served either chilled, warmed, or flaming. For an interesting party idea, set out platters of hot and cold crêpes and assorted fillings, and invite your guests to roll their own.

Appetizer Crêpes

Finger Food Crêpes

1 recipe Eggplant Caviar
  (page 40)
1 recipe Curried Shrimp
  (page 30)
1 recipe Deviled Ham Crêpes
  (page 37)
1 recipe Guacamole (page
  88)
1 recipe Avocado and
  Chicken Liver Pâté (page
  48)

1 recipe Puree of Garlic and
  Garbanzos (page 100)
1 recipe Taramasalata (page
  100)
1 recipe Blue Cheese and
  Apple Crêpes (page 108)

Prepare Crêpes for a Crowd (page 27) and cool. Fold crêpes in quarters, and arrange in overlapping rows on serving platters. Prepare at least 5 of the appetizer fillings or spreads listed above and set in serving bowls. Refrigerate until ready to serve. Arrange dips around the platters of crêpes and let your guests make their own hors d'oeuvres.

Main Dish Crêpe

Baked Lasagne Piedmontese

⅔ cup olive oil
3 large onions, chopped
1 pound mushrooms,
  cleaned and chopped
6 cloves garlic, minced
1 pound hot Italian sausage,
  peeled and crumbled
3 pounds Italian plum to-
  matoes, coarsely chopped

Salt and pepper to taste
2 bay leaves
1 tablespoon oregano
2 teaspoons basil
½ cup tomato paste
2 pounds ricotta cheese
4 eggs, beaten
½ pound grated Parmesan
  cheese

Prepare Crêpes for a Crowd (page 27). Cook onions in hot oil, stirring frequently, until translucent and beginning to brown. Add mushrooms, garlic, and sausage meat. Cook, stirring, until meat loses its pink color. Stir in tomatoes, spices, and tomato paste. Simmer, stirring occasionally, for 1½ hours or until sauce thickens. Mix together ricotta and eggs to make a sauce. *To assemble:* Line 2 lasagne pans with a layer of crêpes. Spread a layer of sauce over the crêpes and top with a layer of crêpes. Now spread on a layer of ricotta cheese mixture and top with another layer of crêpes. Repeat this pattern until all ingredients are used, finishing with a layer of meat sauce. Sprinkle with Parmesan cheese and bake in a moderate oven (350°F.) 45 minutes or until sauce is bubbling hot. Makes enough lasagne for 25 people.

Dessert Crêpes

Chocolate Mousse Crêpes

12 egg whites
3 cups sugar
1 teaspoon cream of tartar
1½ cups water
4 cups semisweet chocolate,
  melted and cooled

¼ cup orange-flavored
  liqueur
3 pints heavy cream, whipped
  stiff
Confectioners' sugar

Prepare Crêpes for a Crowd (page 27), cool, and fold in quarters. Beat egg whites until stiff. Cook sugar, cream of tartar, and water until it reaches the soft ball stage (232°F. on a candy thermometer). Add sugar mixture in a thin stream to egg whites, beating vigorously until cooled. Moisten cooled chocolate mixture with liqueur, fold in whipped cream and egg whites. Raise top flap and fill the pockets of crêpes with mousse, arrange on serving dishes, refrigerate at least 2 hours. Sprinkle with confectioners' sugar. Fills about 60 crêpes.

Lemon Sponge Crêpes

3 cups sugar
1 cup melted butter
1¼ cups sifted flour
Grated rind of 8 lemons
1 cup fresh lemon juice

4 cups milk
8 eggs, separated
1 teaspoon salt
Granulated sugar

Prepare Crêpes for a Crowd (page 27). Mix sugar, butter, flour, lemon rind and juice, milk, and egg yolks in a heavy-bottomed 3-quart saucepan. Cook, stirring constantly, over moderate heat until thickened. Remove from heat, cool. Beat egg whites with salt until stiff but not dry, fold into the lemon mixture. Spoon onto crêpes, roll up, arrange seam side down on oven-proof serving dishes, and sprinkle with sugar. Bake in a moderate oven (350°F.) for 25 minutes. Serve right from the oven or cool. Fills about 60 crêpes.

Crêpes Suzette

1 pound butter, softened
2 cups granulated sugar
Grated rind of 4 oranges and
  2 lemons

Juice of 4 oranges and 4
  lemons
¾ cup orange-flavored
  liqueur
¾ cup brandy or Cognac

Prepare Crêpes for a Crowd (page 27). Cool, fold in quarters, and arrange in overlapping rows on oven-proof serving dishes. Melt butter in a heavy-bottomed 3-quart saucepan. Stir in sugar and orange and lemon rinds, cook, stirring frequently, until caramelized. Stir in orange and lemon juices, continue cooking until sauce is the consistency of heavy cream. At this point, both the crêpes and the sauce (without the liqueur and brandy) may be kept refrigerated until ready to finish. Heat crêpes in a moderately low oven (250°F.) until warmed through. Bring sauce to a boil, remove from heat, and stir in Grand Marnier and brandy. Pour sauce over warm crêpes and set aflame. Makes about 60 crêpes.

Do-It-Yourself Crêpes

2 quarts strawberries
¼ cup orange liqueur
2 quarts orange and/or
  pineapple sections
½ cup superfine sugar

¼ cup brandy
1 pint whipped cream
1 pint yogurt
3 packages (10 oz. each)
  frozen raspberries

Prepare Crêpes for a Crowd (page 27). Wash and hull berries, arrange in serving bowl. Sprinkle with orange liqueur. Cover and refrigerate. Arrange orange and/or pineapple sections in serving bowl. Sprinkle with sugar and brandy. Cover and refrigerate. Combine whipped cream and yogurt for smooth "crème fraîche." Refrigerate. Defrost raspberries and puree in blender. Place in serving bowl with ladle. At serving time, set out cold bowls of filling and toppings and about 60 hot crêpes, on warming trays. Guests add fruit fillings of their choice, roll and top with crème fraîche, raspberry sauce, to taste.

INDEX